LET'S TALK ABOUT IT

AF432825

A Deep Look into the Words of Tupac Shakur

More Than the Music: Open, honest, and objective conversations around the isms of our communities through the timeless lyrics of Tupac Shakur and other prolific writers.

Introduction

Safe space conversations can be the foundation to build bridges between our differences of race, culture, social issues, and all things that affect everyday people. This workbook is intended to help professors and other educators, public leaders, non-profits, community organizers, and the public interested in having the dialogues that can bring about community growth and positive change.

Each chapter contains a Tupac song that we will break down and discuss through conversation and questions. The chapters begin and end with relatable quotes by prolific writers from, Tzu Sun, St. Augustine, and Harriet Tubman to Jay Z, Beyonce, KRS One, Meek Mill and Barack Obama. These quotes are intended to spark our brains into thinking of things greater than ourselves. The challenge would be to ask ourselves, "Why did this person say this?" and "Did it need to be said at all?" What were the conditions that would drive someone to say something so profound?

The goal is to encourage heartfelt dialogue between people from different communities and perspectives that is challenging yet inviting.
Professors and group leaders can use this tool to guide these deep and at times very uncomfortable conversations and differences of opinion in safe space atmospheres without the fear of backlash due to the perception of a position. Incorporating hip-hop lyrics from an artist such as Tupac can aid in the growth of what we have in common and better understand what we don't have in common in a more meaningful way.

Table of Contents

THUG LIFE

"The Hate You Give Little Infants Fucks Everyone"

What Does This Mean to You?

"We ain't doing crimes for the sake of doing crimes, we movin' dimes cause we ain't doing fine. One out of three of us is locked up doing time, do you know what type of shit that can do to a nigga's mind?" - Jay-Z

"I had reasoned this out of my mind. There was one of two things that I had a right to, liberty or death; if I could not have one, I would have the other." - Harriet Tubman

"An individual who breaks a law that his conscience tells him is unjust, and who willingly accepts the penalty of imprisonment in order to arouse the conscience of the community over its injustice, is in reality expressing the highest respect for the law." - Rev. Dr. Martin Luther King, Jr.

"Why you got these kids' minds thinking that they evil, while the Preacher being freaky, you say honor God's people." - Tupac Shakur

"War is just when it is necessary; arms are permissible when there is no hope except in arms." - Niccolo Machiavelli

"Mama, why they keep on calling me nigga? Get my weight up with my hate and pay them back when I'm bigger!" - Tupac Shakur

"Unless we're shooting, no one notices the youth!" - Tupac Shakur

"Never wound a snake, kill it!" - Harriet Tubman

"To nourish children and raise them against odds is in any time, any place, more valuable than to fix bolts in cars or design nuclear weapons." - Marilyn French

"Guess we was evil since birth, product of cursed semen. `Cause even our birthdays are cursed days. A born thug in the first place. The worse way." - Tupac Shakur

Krazy

Makaveli, The Don Killuminati 7 Day Theory

(Intro)
Pass me a cigarette dawg. They got me feelin' crazier than a motherfucker. I got Bad Azz in this motherfucker. Makaveli the Don, representing the Outlawz. Bad Ass representing the LBC.

(Chorus)
Time goes by, puffin on la, hoping that it gets me high. Gotta make you go crazy. I feel crazy.

Last year was a hard one, but life goes on. I hold my head against the wall learning right from wrong. They say my ghetto instrumental, is detrimental to kids, as if they can't see the misery in which they live. Blame me for the outcome, ban my records. Check it! Don't have to bump this but please respect it! I took a minus and now the hard times are behind us, turned into a plus and now they stuck living blinded. Hennessy got me feelin' bad. Time to stop drinking, rolling in my droptop Jag, what's that cop thinking? Sitting in my car watching the stars and smoke, I came a long way but still I got so far to go.

Dear Momma, don't worry, Imma watch for snakes. Tell Sekyiwa that I love her, but it's hard today. I got the letter that she sent me, and I cried for weeks. This is what came out when I tried to speak. All I heard was -

(Chorus)
Time goes by, puffin on la, hoping that it gets me high. Gotta make you go crazy. I feel crazy.

I see Bloods and Crips running up the hill, looking for a better way. My brothers and sisters it's time to build, cause even thug niggas pray. Hoping God hear me! I entered the game, look how much I changed. I'm no longer innocent, casualties in vain. Made a lot of money, seen a lot of places, and I swear I seen the peaceful smile on my momma's face when I gave her keys to her own house. This your land, your only son done became a man. Watching time fly. I love my people do or die. But I wonder why we scared to let each other fly. June 1-6 7-1, the day momma pushed me out her womb, told me "nigga get paid" No one could understand me. The black sheep, outcasted from my family. Now packing heat. I run the streets, a young runaway, live for the day. When I die, will I hear them say -

(Chorus)

Time goes by, puffin on la, hoping that it gets me high. Gotta make you go crazy. I feel crazy.

Let's Talk About it

In this song, Tupac is reaching out to those with a sense of hopelessness. *Krazy* is a very easy to listen to melody, but it also provides familiarity and a complex compassion for the life he describes. Critics may say the song is a bad influence because of Tupac's "smoking on la" and his hopes that it will get him high; however, with a modern perspective, marijuana is no longer seen as an upgrade or "designer" drug such as cocaine, heroin or the new dope "prescription drugs." Marijuana is broadly legal in most states and is the second most popular recreational drug in America.

Tupac took a risk with harsh truths in this work, but that's consistent with and authentic to Tupac across his catalog. He understands firsthand that in order for a person to listen, you must first reach them via truth and relatability. Tupac was a soul speaker, and his fans knew what they were hearing is what Tupac felt. Tupac was selfless in nature and a giant in character and sincerity, who felt an insatiable responsibility for his community.

Krazy addresses the life of someone who has experienced struggle and disappointment. Tupac opens this song by confessing "Last year was a hard one, but life goes on. I hold my head against the wall learning right from wrong." Life can be hard, and it is indeed full of lessons. In these lessons, we learn right from wrong, and it is important to be able to know the difference. One should grow and nurture what is right and do the opposite of what you know to be wrong. Admission of your own role in your circumstance is the first step to moving forward, whether it is from a painful past, recovering from hard times, a mistake made, or the end of work or an intimate relationship. Admission is the first step in healing and the cleansing of the soul. Admission is the oil to the machine called progress.

Discussion

1. Can you recall a time when admission served as a breakthrough to progress and or healing?
2. Can you forgive a person who will not acknowledge that they caused you harm?
3. Have you ever expected to be forgiven without admitting that you caused harm?
4. Discuss a time when you know that you committed an error in your decisions.
5. Have you ever been truly forgiven, but didn't believe it?
6. Have you ever expressed forgiveness, but it was not sincere?

Tupac refers to his music as being "ghetto instrumental." Just as country music or the blues takes your mind to a particular place and lifestyle, Tupac's "ghetto instrumental" does the same, representing the voices of people that experience the ghetto. His voice stands for the forgotten and also speaks of awareness, love and respect for life. There are people trapped in mindsets or situations that are unable to articulate how or what they are feeling, and as a consequence they are unable to admit, heal and move on. There are people who are able to verbalize what they are feeling and thinking. Each of these groups of people can relate to this "ghetto instrumental".

Tupac presents real ghetto stories to the world and proves that they have a rightful place in music, despite the negative assumptions and America's inner, and at times overt, desire to look the other way. Tupac is speaking for these people; he is speaking to these people. Tupac says in his song They Don't Give a Fuck About Us, "Give us chance, help us advance cause we're trying. Ignore our whole plea, watching us in disgust! And they beg when my guns bust. They don't give a fuck about us!"

1. In regard to his music being deemed detrimental, who is the "they" Tupac is referring to
2. Can music be detrimental to children? Why or why not?
3. Do you believe that Tupac's music is detrimental to kids?
4. How can we help children succeed if there are constant negative influences we can't protect them from?
5. Translate what Tupac means in his song *They Don't Give a Fuck About Us* when he says "give us a chance, help us advance cause we're trying. Ignore my whole plea, watching us in disgust. And they beg when my guns bust. They don't give a fuck about us."
6. Do you believe that the government is doing enough for youth groups and social organizations so that real generational progress can be made to minimize violence and poverty?
7. What programs or social groups are in your community that serve the purpose of uplifting disenfranchised people?

Tupac seems to challenge "them" for pretending not to recognize poverty by continuing with this verse; "as if they can't see the misery in which they live, blame me for the outcome, ban my records. Check it! Don't have to bump this but please respect it."

This statement ties back to the previous discussion on admission. The media attempts to blame rap music and rappers for drug use and violence in America. However, there appears to be little fallout for America's own gun manufacturers and transporters who ultimately, and at times brazenly, act as the legal distributor or dealer of the very guns and drugs that are killing our children, destroying families and the lives of people across the globe. In Chris Rock's standup comedy routine *Never Scared*, he states in a roundabout way that when a gun manufacturer makes guns, he is protected by laws and lobbyists, and when a rapper mentions guns, it calls for a professional hearing on Capitol Hill about the damaging effects of rap in America. This contradiction is rooted in imperialism capitalism, which is inherently racist and profiteering. The lack of access to quality education, healthcare and housing, cultivates a culture of dependency and need that prevents social growth and economic freedom and independence.

1. When you see poverty, what feeling does it invoke?
2. How does music bridge ideological and cultural differences?
3. What is the difference in seeing these stories of disadvantage on TV vs. in person?
4. What is the "outcome" Tupac is referring to?
5. How might the censorship of music or literature affect the possibility of it bridging differences and cultures?

Tupac's stance appears to support the constitutional right of free speech, whereas we see on a growing basis, this basic right of democracy being threatened because of small but rising groups that take advantage of the rights intent. He states that it's okay if his music isn't played but his words should be respected.

1. In what ways does Tupac believe his music can be respected?
2. How might you respect something that you do not agree with?
3. What are your overall thoughts on the right of free speech?
4. When should public speaking be punished? Should it ever be punished?

As most people know, Tupac was shot in Las Vegas on September 7, 1996, and died six days later on September 13. This crime remains unsolved. This song was released on Tupac's *The Don Killuminati: The 7 Day Theory* album on November 5, 1996, just two months after Tupac's murder.

There was a community of conspiracy theorists who believe he is in fact still alive and faked his death. Tupac's long standing fan base largely believe wholeheartedly that Tupac wanted his fans to believe that he lives on forever and with that, it is believed that his fans found peace and acceptance in grieving his death. He goes on to say, "I took a minus and now the hard times are behind us, turned into a plus, now they stuck living blinded." Conspiracy theorists believe the use of the word "minus" implies his death and now his hard times are behind him. Tupac turning into a plus; the image of a cross, symbolizes his death and his feeling that he was being crucified by false accusations and beefs that he had in the rap industry. His fan base was left dumbfounded about how and why the life of this messenger was cut short at such a young and vibrant age.

1. Are you aware of the community of people that believe Tupac faked his death?
2. Have you heard of the 7 Day Theory? Tupac was shot on the 7th day at the age of 25 (2+5), pronounced dead at 4:03 pm and his birthday is June 16th (1+6). Also, on his first post humous album, he depicted himself as Jesus crucified on the cross and Jesus, who rose again, had 7 disciples.
3. Have you ever believed in something that was considered a conspiracy theory?
4. Are you open to opposing opinions or facts that challenge your belief systems?
5. Do you follow more than one news source? What are your news sources? Let's talk about it.
6. What would be the purpose of spreading a conspiracy theory that has been proven to be false by independent fact checkers?

Tupac goes on with "Hennessy got me feeling bad, time to stop drinking. Rollin' in my drop top Jag, what's that cop thinking? Sitting in my car watching stars and smoke, I came a long way, but still I got so far to go." This appears to be a moment of self-reflection. In order to grow and learn, we must take the time to evaluate ourselves objectively and reassess the current and future direction of our lives.

Humility even in light of his successes was a characteristic Tupac possessed in spades. In fact, he embraced it, and that is a large part of the reason he was able to reach so many people from so many different walks of life. In the middle of his self-reflection, he makes a point to wonder what the cops are thinking. While self-evaluation is crucial, it is also critical to remain aware of your surroundings at all times.

As a product of the Black Panther movement and growing up in the heart of the Civil Rights Era, Tupac knew all too well to remain aware of police presence and their influence in the community, and he had, like many others mastered that while continuing with his daily activities.

1. What are your observations when you analyze your own life?
2. What bad habits do you have that you'd like to break?
3. Are there any hobbies or interests you'd like to begin? What has kept you from them so far?
4. What is your measurement for happiness in your own life?
5. Do you feel like you live in the present? Or the past, or the future? Explain how.
6. Have you come a long way, do you have a long way to go, or both?
7. At what age, if any, were you talked to about the proper behavior around law enforcement?
8. Have you ever feared a police officer?
9. Has any of your peers expressed having a fear of interacting with law enforcement?

He goes on to say, "Dear Mama, don't worry, I'm a watch for snakes. Tell Sekyiwa, that I love her, but it's hard today. I got the letter that she sent me, and I cried for weeks. This is what came out when I tried to speak". Tupac is one of the first rap artists to express painful emotion in his lyrics, profess his imperfections and his comfort with crying. Men who show emotion are usually looked down as if it shows some kind of weakness. A confident man is comfortable with expressing how he feels, and Tupac was not afraid of such expression, because he was a soul speaker that spoke from his heart. His confessions opened the door for men to feel okay in sharing their true feelings and bring more passionate and honest rappers to the forefront.

1. How do you feel about men crying?

2. Have you ever seen a man feel shame for crying?

3. Have you ever made a man feel bad for crying?

4. Do you know anyone incarcerated?

5. Do you communicate with them? How do you communicate with them?

Tupac lived a long part of his life growing up in Oakland, CA at a time when gangs were prevalent and black on black crime was at its highest rate in American history. In the final verse he refers to these gang members as running up a hill and looking for a better way. Tupac was often ridiculed and accused by the masses and the media of glorifying gang life, but if you listen to his lyrics, you may see that accusation is far from the truth.

His reference to running up a hill can be representative of a tiring process that goes against the laws of gravity and the rule of law. Gang life is not gratifying, rather exhausting at best. He goes on to say that they are looking for a "better way." Again, he is stating that they are looking for a better way of living, loving, and achieving their ultimate goal, which is to live free, be respected and protected by the laws of their own land.

Tupac stated in his song *Me Against the World*, "Can't reach the children cause they illin'. Addicted to the killing and the appeal of the cap peelin'. Without feelin', but will they last or be blasted? Hardheaded bastard, maybe you'll listen in this casket, the aftermath. More bodies being buried, I'm missing my homies in a hurry they relocating to the cemetery." It is clear where the ultimate road to gang life leads you, jail, addicted, or dead. The rate of new gang members and supremacy groups is growing higher and higher each day and we must ask ourselves why. There are thousands of street and supremacy gang members and victims of this warfare that have been taken from families who never would have thought it would happen to them.

1. Do you view gang life as a choice or a necessity?

2. Do you view supremacy gangs as a choice or a necessity?

3. Does the lifestyle depend on geographic location and economic conditions?

4. Does lifestyle depend on race?

5. If you were born into a gang ridden area, what would you do to avoid joining a gang?

6. If you were born into a family "of supreme race" because it is understood amongst them that their race is supreme to the others and are afforded more rights due to this, what would you do to manage this ideology and this "entitlement"?

7. Do you believe that gang members can have a spiritual connection to God?

8. Do you believe that supremacist gangs have a spiritual connection to God?

9. Do you believe God hears the prayers of these gang members?

Some may argue that the upside to gang life and drug dealing is the gain of economic power. It provides those born without much, the ability to buy their clothes and food and may allow a young teenager to pay rent on behalf of their low income, or uneducated, possibly drug addicted parents. Let us not forget the generations of our 70's and 80's mothers that became grandmothers, raising their crack addicted children's kids. These children are parents now, raising their own, pulling from the manner in which they were raised.

The combination of all these conditions on top of a rundown home, poor educational systems, healthcare and little to no supervision due to parents overworking or simply not caring, creates the vacuum we are losing our children in. Tupac says in his song *My Block*, "I can't blame the dealers, my momma's welfare check, bought the next man chrome wheels." In other words, there would not be a supply if it were not for the demand, simple economics.

The same theory can be applied to hatred. There would be no supply for hate if there were not a demand. Though the means of making quick cash or reputation may bring temporary feelings of accomplishment, the flip side is it nothing other than genocide. It is reported that over 45% of murders in America are drug related. Tupac goes on to state in this song "made a lot of money, seen a lot of places, and I swear I seen a peaceful smile on my momma's face when I gave her the keys to her own house, this your land. Your only son done became a man."

In Tupac's case, he was able to provide for his mother in this manner by living a legal lifestyle, making songs that sold millions. He traveled the world starting out with the Digital Underground and became successful after his collaboration on the group's song titled *Same Song*. His first album, the most political and unfortunately, the least successful, introduced him to the world as a young talented rapper on the rise, with a whole lot to say.

1. Would you ever accept an extravagant gift from a person who may have obtained the cash to buy it by illegal means?
2. Does the acceptance of such gifts contribute to these lifestyles?
3. Do you believe that illegal and legal drug use contributes to drug warfare?
4. How do the laws of supply and demand relate to drug use and illegal drug trade?
5. How do the laws of supply and demand relate to hate?

Tupac closes his verse in this song by saying "No one can understand me, the black sheep outcasted from my family, now packing heat. I run the streets a young runaway, live for the day. When I die, I can hear them say?" The feeling of being misunderstood is aggravating at best but when it is combined with extreme race and class differences it can be destructive.

Most families have a "black sheep," where one or more relatives are not walking in the same path as the others. A black sheep in the family can be a product of wealth or poverty; this stigma does not discriminate, and this is usually due to them feeling different or misunderstood. An extreme introvert may prefer solitude. A molested child may act out by way of promiscuity, drug use, or violence. A child who is treated poorly in comparison to their siblings may act out in a way that is unpleasing to an adult. A child born into poverty may react in a way that is not pleasing to society and to go even further, children born into poverty tend to suffer from moderate to severe health conditions such as asthma, emotional distress or a tendency towards violence which makes getting along even more of a challenge.

Over 1.5 million children in America are homeless and living on the streets or in shelters. As mentioned previously, when a pain is not articulated well, it falls subject to assumptions, closed minds and unfounded rumors and opinions, which becomes the gateway to being misunderstood and possibly destructive. Being misunderstood loses out on compassion but wins in being ignored and mislabeled. Tupac was so relatable because people from all walks of life identified with him, no matter the race, religion or social class.

1. Talk about a time when you felt misunderstood.

2. When faced with evaluating someone's behavior, how do you try to understand their motivation?

3. Have you ever spoken to a homeless person? What was their story?

4. What is the future for a young runaway?

5. Where will the misunderstood ultimately fit within society?

6. What is the risk to your community when you don't try to understand your neighbor?

7. What is the benefit to your community when we try to understand our differences in culture and ideology?

Time Period Reference Photos

The Black Panther May 15, 1967 — PAGE THREE

FUNCTIONAL DEFINITION OF POLITICS.

BY HUEY P. NEWTON

Politics is war without bloodshed. War is politics with bloodshed. Politics has its particular characteristics which differentiate it from war. When the peaceful means of politics are exhausted and the people do not get what they want, politics are continued. Usually it ends up in physical conflict which is called war, which is also political.

Because we lack political power, black people are not free. Black reconstruction failed because black people did not have political and military power. The masses of black people at the time were very clear on the definition of political power. It is evident in the songs of black people at that time. In the songs it was stated that on the Day of Jubilee we'd have forty acres and two mules. This was promised black people by the Freedman's Bureau. This was freedom as far as the black masses were concerned.

The Talented Tenth at the time viewed freedom as operative in the political arena. Black people did operate in the political arena during reconstruction. They were more educated than most of the whites in the south. They had been educated in France, Canada and England, and were very qualified to serve in the political arena. But yet, Black Reconstruction failed.

When one operates in the political arena, it is assumed that he has power or represents

(continued on page 4)

MINISTER OF DEFENSE

HUEY P. NEWTON

FEAR AND DOUBT

BY HUEY P. NEWTON

The lower socio-economic BLACK male is a man of confusion. He faces a hostile environment and is not sure that it is not his own sins that have attracted the hostilities of society. All his life he has been taught (explicitly and implicitly) that he is an inferior approximation of humanity. As a man, he finds himself void of those things that bring respect and a feeling of worthiness. He looks around for something to blame for his situation, but because he is not sophisticated regarding the socio-economic millieu and because of negativistic parental and institutional teachings he ultimately blames himself. When he was a child, his parents told him that they were not affluent because "we didn't have the opportunity to become educated", or "we did not take advantage of the educational opportunities that were offered us". They tell the child that things will be different for him if he is educated and skilled, but there is absolutely nothing other than this occassional warning (and often not even this) to stimulate education. BLACK people are great worshippers of education, even the lower socio-economic BLACK person, but at the same time he is afraid to expose himself to it. he is afraid because he is vulnerable to having his fears verified; perhaps he will find that he can't compete with white students. He tells himself that he could have done it if he had really wanted to. The fact is, of course, that the assumed educational opportun-

(continued on page 4)

(continued on page 4)

WHAT WE WANT NOW!   WHAT WE BELIEVE

TO THOSE POOR SOULS WHO DON'T KNOW BLACK HISTORY, THE BELIEFS AND DESIRES OF THE BLACK PANTHER PARTY FOR SELF DEFENSE MAY SEEM UNREASONABLE. TO BLACK PEOPLE, THE TEN POINTS COVERED ARE ABSOLUTELY ESSENTIAL TO SURVIVAL. WE HAVE LISTENED TO THE RIOT PRODUCING WORDS "THESE THINGS TAKE TIME" FOR 400 YEARS. THE BLACK PANTHER PARTY KNOWS WHAT BLACK PEOPLE WANT AND NEED. BLACK UNITY AND SELF DEFENSE WILL MAKE THESE DEMANDS A REALITY.

WHAT WE WANT

1. WE WANT FREEDOM. WE WANT POWER TO DETERMINE THE DESTINY OF OUR BLACK COMMUNITY.

2. WE WANT FULL EMPLOYMENT FOR OUR PEOPLE.

3. WE WANT AN END TO THE ROBBERY BY THE WHITE MAN OF OUR BLACK COMMUNITY.

4. WE WANT DECENT HOUSING, FIT FOR SHELTER HUMAN BEINGS.

5. WE WANT EDUCATION FOR OUR PEOPLE THAT EXPOSES THE TRUE NATURE OF THIS DECADENT AMERICAN SOCIETY. WE WANT EDUCATION THAT TEACHES US OUR TRUE HISTORY AND OUR ROLE IN THE PRESENT DAY SOCIETY.

6. WE WANT ALL BLACK MEN TO BE EXEMPT FROM MILITARY SERVICE.

7. WE WANT AN IMMEDIATE END TO POLICE BRUTALITY AND MURDER OF BLACK PEOPLE.

8. WE WANT FREEDOM FOR ALL BLACK MEN HELD IN FEDERAL, STATE, COUNTY, AND CITY PRISONS AND JAILS.

9. WE WANT ALL BLACK PEOPLE WHEN BROUGHT TO TRIAL TO BE TRIED IN COURT BY A JURY OF THEIR PEER GROUP OR PEOPLE FROM THEIR BLACK COMMUNITIES. AS DEFINED BY THE CONSTITUTION OF THE UNITED STATES.

10. WE WANT LAND, BREAD, HOUSING, EDUCATION, CLOTHING, JUSTICE AND PEACE.

WHAT WE BELIEVE

1. WE BELIEVE THAT BLACK PEOPLE WILL NOT BE FREE UNTIL WE ARE ABLE TO DETERMINE OUR DESTINY.

2. WE BELIEVE THAT THE FEDERAL GOVERNMENT IS RESPONSIBLE AND OBLIGATED TO GIVE EVERY MAN EMPLOYMENT OR A GUARANTEED INCOME. WE BELIEVE THAT IF THE WHITE AMERICAN BUSINESS MEN WILL NOT GIVE FULL EMPLOYMENT, THEN THE MEANS OF PRODUCTION SHOULD BE TAKEN FROM THE BUSINESS MEN AND PLACED IN THE COMMUNITY SO THAT THE PEOPLE OF THE COMMUNITY CAN ORGANIZE AND EMPLOY ALL OF ITS PEOPLE AND GIVE A HIGH STANDARD OF LIVING.

3. WE BELIEVE THAT THIS RACIST GOVERNMENT HAS ROBBED US AND NOW WE ARE DEMANDING THE OVERDUE DEBT OF FORTY ACRES AND TWO MULES. FORTY ACRES AND TWO MULES WAS PROMISED 100 YEARS AGO AS RETRIBUTION FOR SLAVE LABOR AND MASS MURDER OF BLACK PEOPLE. WE WILL ACCEPT THE PAYMENT IN CURRENCY WHICH WILL BE DISTRIBUTED TO OUR MANY COMMUNITIES. THE GERMANS ARE NOW AIDING THE JEWS IN ISRAEL FOR THE GENOCIDE OF THE JEWISH PEOPLE. THE GERMANS MURDERED 6,000,000 JEWS. THE AMERICAN RACIST HAS TAKEN PART IN THE SLAUGHTER OF OVER 50,000,000 BLACK PEOPLE; THEREFORE, WE FEEL THAT THIS IS A MODEST DEMAND THAT WE MAKE.

4. WE BELIEVE THAT IF THE WHITE LANDLORDS WILL NOT GIVE DECENT HOUSING TO OUR BLACK COMMUNITY, THEN THE HOUSING AND THE LAND SHOULD BE MADE INTO COOPERATIVES SO THAT OUR COMMUNITY, WITH GOVERNMENT AID, CAN BUILD AND MAKE DECENT HOUSING FOR ITS PEOPLE.

5. WE BELIEVE IN AN EDUCATIONAL SYSTEM THAT WILL GIVE TO OUR PEOPLE A KNOWLEDGE OF SELF. IF A MAN DOES NOT HAVE KNOWLEDGE OF HIMSELF AND HIS POSITION IN SOCIETY AND THE WORLD, THEN HE HAS LITTLE CHANCE TO RELATE TO ANYTHING ELSE.

6. WE BELIEVE THAT BLACK PEOPLE SHOULD NOT BE FORCED TO FIGHT IN THE MILITARY SERVICE TO DEFEND A RACIST GOVERNMENT THAT DOES NOT PROTECT US. WE WILL NOT FIGHT AND KILL OTHER PEOPLE OF COLOR IN THE WORLD WHO, LIKE BLACK PEOPLE, ARE BEING VICTIMIZED BY THE WHITE RACIST GOVERNMENT OF AMERICA. WE WILL PROTECT OURSELVES FROM THE FORCE AND VIOLENCE OF THE RACIST POLICE AND THE RACIST MILITARY, BY WHATEVER MEANS NECESSARY.

7. WE BELIEVE WE CAN END POLICE BRUTALITY IN OUR BLACK COMMUNITY BY ORGANIZING BLACK SELF DEFENSE GROUPS THAT ARE DEDICATED TO DEFENDING OUR BLACK COMMUNITY FROM RACIST POLICE OPPRESSION AND BRUTALITY. THE SECOND AMENDMENT OF THE CONSTITUTION OF THE UNITED STATES GIVES US A RIGHT TO BEAR ARMS. WE THEREFORE BELIEVE THAT ALL BLACK PEOPLE SHOULD ARM THEMSELVES FOR SELF DEFENSE.

8. WE BELIEVE THAT ALL BLACK PEOPLE SHOULD BE RELEASED FROM THE MANY JAILS AND PRISONS BECAUSE THEY HAVE NOT RECEIVED A FAIR AND IMPARTIAL TRIAL.

9. WE BELIEVE THAT THE COURTS SHOULD FOLLOW THE UNITED STATES CONSTITUTION SO THAT BLACK PEOPLE WILL RECEIVE FAIR TRIALS. THE 14TH AMENDMENT OF THE U.S. CONSTITUTION GIVES A MAN A RIGHT TO BE TRIED BY HIS PEER GROUP. A PEER IS A PERSON FROM A SIMILAR ECONOMIC, SOCIAL, RELIGIOUS, GEOGRAPHICAL, ENVIRONMENTAL, HISTORICAL AND RACIAL BACKGROUND. TO DO THIS THE COURT WILL BE FORCED TO SELECT A JURY FROM THE BLACK COMMUNITY FROM WHICH THE BLACK DEFENDANT CAME. WE HAVE BEEN, AND ARE BEING TRIED BY ALL WHITE JURIES THAT HAVE NO UNDERSTANDING OF THE "AVERAGE REASONING MAN" OF THE BLACK COMMUNITY.

10. WHEN IN THE COURSE OF HUMAN EVENTS, IT BECOMES NECESSARY FOR ONE PEOPLE TO DISSOLVE THE POLITICAL BONDS WHICH HAVE CONNECTED THEM WITH ANOTHER, AND TO ASSUME AMONG THE POWERS OF THE EARTH, THE SEPARATE AND EQUAL STATION TO WHICH THE LAWS OF NATURE AND NATURE'S GOD ENTITLE THEM, A DECENT RESPECT TO THE OPINIONS OF MANKIND REQUIRES THAT THEY SHOULD DECLARE THE CAUSES WHICH IMPEL THEM TO SEPARATION. WE HOLD THESE TRUTHS TO BE SELF-EVIDENT, THAT ALL MEN ARE CREATED EQUAL, THAT THEY ARE ENDOWED BY THEIR CREATOR WITH CERTAIN INALIENABLE RIGHTS, THAT AMONG THESE ARE LIFE, LIBERTY AND THE PURSUIT OF HAPPINESS. THAT TO SECURE THESE RIGHTS, GOVERNMENTS ARE INSTITUTED AMONG MEN, DERIVING THEIR JUST POWERS FROM THE CONSENT OF THE GOVERNED, - THAT WHENEVER ANY FORM OF GOVERNMENT BECOMES DESTRUCTIVE OF THESE ENDS, IT IS THE RIGHT OF PEOPLE TO ALTER OR TO ABOLISH IT, AND TO INSTITUTE NEW GOVERNMENT, LAYING ITS FOUNDATION ON SUCH PRINCIPLES AND ORGANIZING ITS POWERS IN SUCH FORM AS TO THEM SHALL SEEM MOST LIKELY TO EFFECT THEIR SAFETY AND HAPPINESS.

PRUDENCE, INDEED, WILL DICTATE THAT GOVERNMENTS LONG ESTABLISHED SHOULD NOT BE CHANGED FOR LIGHT AND TRANSIENT CAUSES; AND ACCORDINGLY ALL EXPERIENCE HATH SHEWN, THAT MANKIND ARE MORE DISPOSE TO SUFFER, WHILE EVILS ARE SUFFERABLE, THAN TO RIGHT THEMSELVES BY ABOLISHING THE FORMS TO WHICH THEY ARE ACCUSTOMED. BUT WHEN A LONG TRAIN OF ABUSES AND USURPATIONS, PURSUING INVARIABLY THE SAME OBJECT, EVINCES A DESIGN TO REDUCE THEM UNDER ABSOLUTE DESPOTISM, IT IS THEIR RIGHT, IT IS THEIR DUTY, TO THROW OFF SUCH GOVERNMENT, AND TO PROVIDE NEW GUARDS FOR THEIR FUTURE SECURITY.

"THE SPIRIT OF THE PEOPLE IS GREATER THAN THE MAN'S TECHNOLOGY"
HUEY P. NEWTON, MINISTER OF DEFENSE, B.P.P.S.D.

THE BLACK PANTHER

Black Community News Service

VOL. V NO. 8   SATURDAY, AUGUST 24, 1970

PUBLISHED WEEKLY   **THE BLACK PANTHER PARTY**   MINISTRY OF INFORMATION BOX 2967, CUSTOM HOUSE SAN FRANCISCO, CA 94126

25 cents

"IF THE PENALTY FOR THE QUEST FOR FREEDOM IS DEATH---THEN BY DEATH WE ESCAPE TO FREEDOM."

HUEY P. NEWTON
SUPREME COMMANDER
BLACK PANTHER PARTY

STORY CENTERFOLD

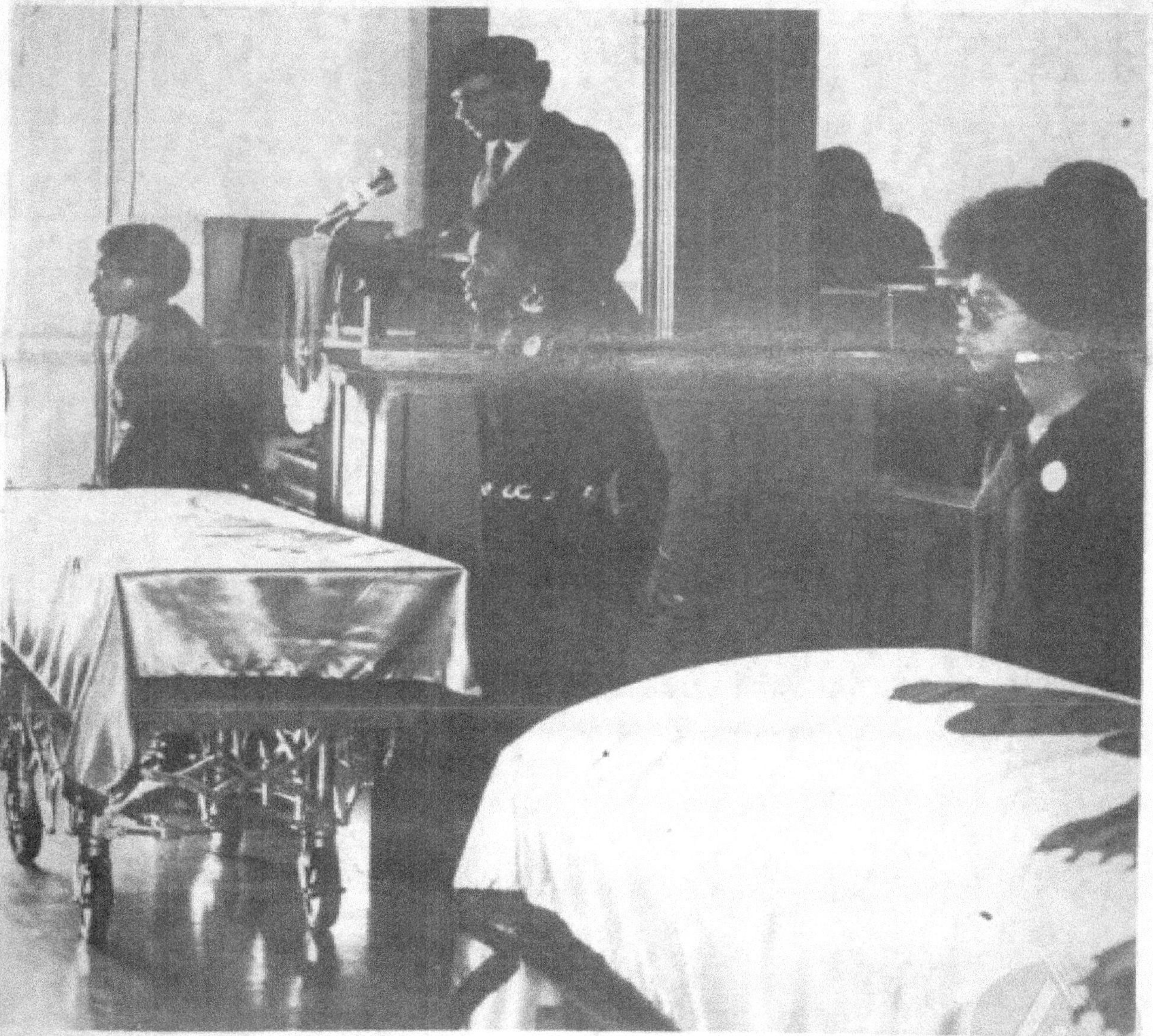

INSIDE: WELFARE OPPRESSION IN MOUNT VERNON, N.Y.   THE PENTAGON...BY MICHAEL "CETEWAYO" TABOR   LETTER FROM HUEY ABOUT THE WOMEN'S LIBERATION AND GAY LIBERATION MOVEMENTS

REPORT ON THE TRIAL OF LONNIE McLUCAS   THE SOLEDAD 15

RACE-OR-CLASS DEBATE
RAGES AMONG "WHITE ORGANIZERS"

KNOXVILLE, Tenn.—Members of many groups working among white people across the nation met at Highlander Center for three days in early March. The gathering had been stimulated by IFCO, the Interreligious-Foundation for Community Organizing.

The 50 persons present tried to decide whether racism is a disease in itself or a symptom of a deeper disorder. White Southerners of working-class origin insisted that racial division is a means of social control, invented and used by the people who own and run the South and the nation.

The conference set up a continuations committee of three men and three women to try to form a national organization to tie together the work of all the groups. The equal division by sex resulted from proposals by a caucus of the women present.

The conference had opened with a statement by Frank Joyce, Detroit, national director of People Against Racism (PAR). He said: "We as whites must seek to make a revolution. We aspire to do this because we have no other option. This society hasn't any idea how to distribute its wealth; it does know how *not* to distribute it. There is no courage, no humanity available to us within this society. It is only in struggle against this society that we find our courage and humanity.

"It is a little presumptuous and pretentious for us to talk about revolution simply because we've been brought up to believe

our problem.

"The problem is the economic system under which we live. Racism, poverty, war are the symptoms of that system. Industrialists and big landowners have always used race in the South to divide people and make more profits; now they are using it nationally."

Braden insisted that any organizing of white people must be done with the aim of forming coalitions with black people; otherwise, there is danger of forming groups which will bolster

organize—how do you get to 2,000 people with your theories? We've got to do some pruning; separate the wheat from the chaff; separate those people who want to talk and those who want to work. I'm not in anti-racist work; I'm trying to organize a movement."

Braden added, "You've got to have guts to free people. If you don't have it and you want to talk to yourself, then you should abandon your projects and quit kidding yourself."

Doug Youngblood, a white Alabamian from the Poor People's Embassy, asked, "What is white? There are millions of whites who ain't got a blonde, blue-eyed wife and a convertible and eating Post Toasties for breakfast. I'm sick of hearing crap like that. I'm not that type of white, neither are millions of others.

"I think it's ridiculous to go into a community and say I'm fighting racism. I want to establish a socialist America. I want a just and a decent society and you can't have that under capitalism. I'm sick of middle-class people defining the problems and tactics for me."

Charles Bevel, a native of Mississippi, added: "Black people are under the illusion that white people are free. Capitalists will always use race to destroy any coalition-organizing work."

National Organizing Committee, told Fields, "You are missing the whole point when you overlook the economic reasons and class structure. In your speech you said police brutality is racism; how do you explain police brutality against whites? How do you explain Chicago? Until you attack the whole system and unless we organize around a class basis against the system, we are not getting anywhere."

Whites Equally Exploited

Youngblood agreed. "I'm from southern Alabama and my people are just as exploited as blacks. This man (Fields) is saying that his degradation is unique because he's black — I say that's bullshit. My people have been just as degraded. Black people ain't going to get free by putting them into the belly of the monster that's devouring us all!"

An organizer from Durham's ACT project, Lawrence Kelly, said, "I grew up in East Texas and I was aware of a prejudice against poor whites before I was aware of a prejudice against 'Negroes."

Finally Bob Zellner asked Dr. Fields, "Do you believe in the capitalist system?" Fields laughed, said he had to catch a plane, and exited.

Eventually people got around to actual work in which they were involved. Some of this dealt with research, some of it took the form of staff workers

spark must come from inside. The total solution, I believe, is the abolition of the capitalist system."

Frank Adams, coordinator of the Virginia Council on Human Relations, talked about his efforts to persuade St. Stephen's Episcopal Church in Richmond to do something about slums. Adams said the chief slumlords in the city attend the church and the church itself owns $50 million worth of tax-exempt property.

"The church is no better than any corporation in its pursuit of profits," he said. Adams' activities were the result of a staff organization and he said he had no constituency. He did point out that Vistas are working on community organizing in conjunction with the program.

Anibal Solivan, a Puerto Rican from New York, criticized the practice of working with Vistas. "These Vista missionaries go into a neighborhood for a year and then leave, and they make my job more difficult when I try to convince people that organizing projects take 20, 30 years," he said.

On the final morning of the conference, the whole question of freedom for women exploded in the midst of the gathering. The nine women present met separately in caucus, and later informed the men that they felt the conference had ignored them as people and had refused to deal with the question of how

(Lyrics to)

White Man'z World

Makaveli, The Don Killuminati 7 Day Theory

(Intro)

Nothin' but love for you my sister.

You know how hard it is to being a woman,

A black woman at that? In this white man'z world.

Sometimes we overlook the fact that we be ridin'

Hard in our shit and we don't be knowing' the pain

we be causing. In this white man'z world.

I aint saying I am innocent of all this.

I'm just saying this song is for yall! For all the times

that I messed up, or we messed up.

Dear sister, got me twisted up in prison, I miss ya. Crying looking at my niece's and nephew's picture. They say don't let this cruel world get ya kind of suspicious, swearing one day you might leave me for somebody that's richer. I twist the cap off the bottle, take a sip and see tomorrow, gotta make it if I have to beg or borrow. Reading love letters late night, locked down and quiet. If brothers don't receive their mail best believe we riot. Eating jack macks and staring at the walls of silence. Inside this cage where they capture all my rage and violence! In time I learned a few lessons, never fall for riches, apologies to my true sisters, far from bitches. Help me raise my black nation; reparations are due it's true. Caught up in this world, I took advantage of you. So tell the babies how I love them. Precious boys and girls, born black, in this white man's world.

Who knows what tomorrow brings, in a world where

everyone lies. Where to go, no matter how far I find,

---

to let you know you're not alone.

Being born with less, I must confess, only adds on to the stress. Two gunshots to my homie's head, died in his vest. Shot him to death, left him bleeding for his family to see. I pass his casket, gently ask him, "is there a heaven for G's?" My homeboy is doing life, his baby momma be stressing. Shedding tears when her son finally asks that question, "Where my daddy at? Mommy why we live so poor? Heard you crying late night through the bedroom door. Do you love me momma, why they keep on calling me nigger?" Get my weight up with my hate and pay 'em back when I bigger! I'm still thuggin' in this jail cell, missing my block. Hearing brothers screaming all night, wishing they'd stop. Proud to be black but why we act like we don't love ourselves? Don't look around brother, check yourself! Know what it means to be black, whether man or girl, we're still struggling in this white man'z world!

Fight song for our political prisoner! We must fight!

So tell me why you changed and choose a new direction, in a blink of an eye. My time away just made perfection. Did you think I died? Not gonna cry, why should I care, like we holding on to lost loves that's no longer there. Can you please help me? God bless me please, keep my seeds healthy, making all my enemies bleed while my G's wealthy. Hoping you bury me with ammunition, weed and shells. Just in case they trip in heaven ain't no G's in hell. Sister sorry for the pain that I caused your heart. I know I'll change if you help me, but don't fall apart. Rest in peace to Latasha, little Yummy and Kado, too much for this cold world to take, ended up being fatal. Every woman in America, especially black, bear with me, can't you see that we're under attack? I never meant to cause drama, to my sister and momma. I hope we make it to better times in this white man'z world.

Never that! In this white man'z world. They can't stop us. We been here all this time and they ain't took us out. They can never take us out! No matter what they say about us being extinct, about us being an endangered species, we ain't never gonna leave this! We ain't never gonna walk off this planet unless y'all choose to! Use your brain! Use your brain! It ain't them that killing us, it's us that's killing us. It ain't them that's knocking us off, it's us that's knocking us off. I'm telling you. You better watch it! Or be a victim, in this white man'z world. In this white man'z world. Born black, in this white man'z world!

No doubt! This is dedicated to my motherfucken teachers; Mutulo Shakur, Geronimo Pratt, Mumia Abu Jamal, Sekou Odingo, all the real OG's, we out!"

Let's Talk About it

One can't help but be impressed by Tupac's passion and his honesty in communicating his innermost thoughts. In this piece, Tupac is reflecting on his upbringing in the political activism sphere and on the harsh reality of the penal system. With his self-reflective abilities, including outright apologies and admissions of fault, he takes us on a journey into the mind of a non-white person living in a "white man'z world."

He has chosen to document his role as an inmate, and with great intensity he guides us through the daily life of prison and explains the emotional turbulence that prisoners live, while embracing varied emotions such as grief, regret, anger, denial, expectations, sorrow, and bitterness. He has put it all on the table for us, and you can hear it when you take in his voice and passion. Tupac as the inmate is writing a letter, expressing the common feelings of sadness, the longing for loved ones, the agony that family separation creates and the insecurity of feeling forgotten.

According to the US Department of Justice in 2018, 6.4 million people were in prison or jail, on parole or probation. According to The Sentencing Project, an organization working to improve fairness and efficacy of criminal justice systems while providing non-jail alternatives, in that same year 2,272 black males for every 100,000 were locked up in state, federal, and local jails. Hispanic representation was 1,018, while white males lost 392 out of 100,000 men sentenced to jails and prisons. The likelihood of lifetime sentences for all men is 1 in 9, but for white men it is only 1 in 17, 1 in 3 for black men, and 1 in 6 for Latinos. One out of 56 women are jailed, but for white women it is nearly double at 1 in 111, while 1 in 18 black women and 1 in 45 Latinas are imprisoned. There is a clear disparity, and while recently there has been increased call for prison reform, only time can measure tangible actions.

Between 2016 and 2020, the US government filled a record number of judicial positions with appointments with little to no experience as judges or even as trial lawyers. Critics believe these judges were installed to return to White Power and Jim Crow values, giving the judicial system even more power to violate the rights of not just black and brown people, but those of other groups such as immigrants, LGBTQIA+ populations, and simply anti-racist people who care about the country's moral fabric and people of all colors. Supporters of these judicial appointments see it as move to restore America back to its original traditional values.

The penal system was originally established to punish an offender for a particular crime, or arguably to control a person or people to force expected behaviors. Pre-civilization punishments were used to serve a dual purpose. The first was public humiliation, where a person charged with a crime would be disciplined in front of a mass of people. The punishments would range from being held in a cage in the raging sun without food, or water, starving, dying a slow and painful death, public mutilation, exile from their community, and torture. This medieval era period in America created the foundation and historical reference for the structure and design of our generation's penal systems. The second purpose was to establish order, so that the Heads of State, i.e. kings and queens, would maintain their empire and preserve power of their land.

As society became more civil, these public punishments became either unnecessary because the desired law and order had been established or it was deemed barbaric. The Americas had also established independence from Britain in 1776 and moved toward a democratic society geared toward European growth and expansion only.

Crime and punishment are very subjective, and therefore cannot be 100% fair and just. A crime to one person may not carry the same weight if judged by another person, nor the appropriate punishment. Nonetheless, even in this century, the establishment and enforcement of law and order is still a necessary requirement. The divisive factors are the excessive force and imbalanced justice, with politicians, police, judges and wardens who cross the line from law-abiding enforcers believing in the wheels of Democracy to criminals themselves.

Does prison really rehabilitate? Many say it does not. Many believe it is all about profit, control, and greed with no real desire for peace and more about selfish power and job security.

Discussion

In the first verse of this song, Tupac almost immediately mentions the damage of human isolation and the importance of communication from the outside world.

1. What real thoughts have you ever given to a prisoner's emotions?
2. Why is mail or any form of communication important to an inmate?
3. Do you have a friend or family member in jail? How often do you think about them? How often do you let them know they are thought of?
4. If you have never experienced this, reflect on how you would handle this situation?

Within the same verse Tupac states "In time I learned a few lessons, never fall for riches, apologies to my true sisters far from bitches." Tupac spoke of females and depicted them in various ways, from strong intelligent queens worthy of protection to being called scandalous hos, tricks, and bitches.

1. Is this a contradiction or is he describing different kinds of women?
2. Can you accept Tupac's opinion that there are females worthy of praise and that there are females deserving criticism?
3. Is there a time when it is okay to disrespect a woman? When and why or why not?
4. Do you know how to apologize?

Tupac never tried to suggest he is perfect. In fact, he admits the errors of his ways often. St. Augustine once said "Do you wish to be great? Then begin by being. Do you desire to construct a vast and lofty fabric? Think first about the foundations of humility. The higher your structure is to be, the deeper must be its foundation."

Humility is the perfect teacher and healer for progression and forward movement. Denial and omission freezes your soul and spirit in the very place in time where your denial began. Moving on is impossible until humility and honesty are permitted. Tupac closes out this verse by saying, "Help me raise my black nation, reparations are due, it's true. Caught up in this world, I took advantage of you. So tell the babies that I love them, precious boys and girls, born black, in this white man'z world."

1. Do mothers of black and brown children have to parent different than those children that are not?
2. Are reparations due? If so, to whom? What are appropriate reparations in the modern era?
3. To whom do you think he is speaking to? African Americans or Native Americans?
4. Has being "caught up" ever made you take advantage of someone or something? Have you made amends for it?
5. Have you ever been taken advantage of? Do you want that person to acknowledge the pain or disappointment they may have caused?

While Tupac has identified a lot of sources of pride, reality and pain in this song, he ends this song as a battle cry, a call to all of those that live without understanding, as many of us subconsciously do. It is a call to those who walk through their own lives not realizing the impact, importance, and contradictions of their own selves. He is thinking about people and things other than himself. He is speaking of his inmate family, their civilian family, the children, the criminal, addicts and of society itself.

Tupac's clear and poignant articulation of life's ills in this song sums up an entire generation's inner thoughts, known and unknown, admitted and denied. I don't believe at all that Tupac is only speaking to black people, but rather to all oppressed. He wants us all to remember, both the powerful and powerless, that we are God's children.

We must remember, at the time this song was written, Tupac was not poor. His will and work ethic had allowed him to acquire the wealth he only dreamed of during those hungry nights as a child.   He never forgot the plight of his ancestors, living poor, and being called a nigger by people in authority.

Poverty is a memory that can never be erased. His lyrics remind us that poverty's effects are everlasting. They vary from person to person, but nevertheless, they are still there. It may keep some of us stuck and hopeless, or it can become the driving force behind some of the most successful people in the world. "Being born with less" is a constant reminder that your starting line in life is so far behind the others you are expected to compete against. How can that person win that race?

1. Are we a product of our society? Or do you believe our society is a product of us?
2. What do you think about the life and mentality of the young man that wears a bulletproof vest?
3. Have you ever had a friend that was murdered? How do you think it affected you going forward?
4. What can make a person feel that death is better than life?
5. How would you react if a teacher insulted your child's intelligence?
6. Imagine being of the times when calling a black child a nigger, stupid, or worthless, was acceptable in our school and judicial systems. What happens when these abused children become parents and members of our society?
7. Tupac said, "Momma why they keep on calling me nigger, get my weight up with my hate and pay 'em back when I'm bigger". What could "pay 'em back" mean? It could mean revenge, a revolution, it could mean becoming self- destructive, it could mean war. It could also mean the birth of activism or making yourself a millionaire like Meek Mill

and Jay Z with their driving spirit being and impoverished past. What does it mean to you?

In this song Tupac demonstrates compassion for people; his legacy will remain as long as the human can feel, touch and see. Whether you agree with his approach or not, whether you take the time to measure this man over his entire lifespan or you pick him apart, he leaves an impact. He leaves you with an opinion.

Tupac knows the children are listening to him. He wrote in his song *They Don't Give a Fuck About Us*, "If I choose to ride, thuggin' to the day I die, nobody gives a fuck about us, but when I start to rise, a hero in their children's eyes, now they give a fuck about us."

Tupac often spoke of his love for women, so he continues to say "Sister sorry for the pain that I caused your heart. I know I will change if you help me, but don't fall apart". Women are often complimented for being the backbone of their men, or the matriarch of our family. However, women's rights have been slow and steady at best and still questioned or attacked.

1. Are there women in your life that you look up to?
2. Should women have the same rights as men?
3. Should women have the right to vote?
4. Should woman have a right to divorce?
5. Should women have a right to make their own medical decisions?

What Does This Mean to You II?

"I ain't a killer but don't push me, revenge is like the sweetest joy next to getting pussy!"
Tupac Shakur

"We ain't thugs for the sake of being thugs, nobody do that where we grew at, nigga duhh. The poverty line we not above, so we come with masks and gloves cause we ain't feeling the love." - Jay-Z

"We probably in hell already, our dumb asses not knowin'. Everybody kissing ass to go to heaven ain't going!" - Tupac Shakur

"Did you hear about the rose that grew from a crack in the concrete? Proving nature's laws wrong. It learned to walk without having feet. Funny it seems, but by keeping its dreams, it learned to breathe fresh air. Long live the rose that grew from concrete when no one else ever cared." - Tupac Shakur

"Men are driven by two principal impulses, either by love or by fear." - Machiavelli

"You can't help it. An artist's duty, as far as I am concerned is to reflect the times." - Nina Simone

"If we have no peace, it is because we have forgotten that we belong to each other." – Mother Theresa

"I swear to the Lord, I still can't see why Democracy means everybody but me." - Langston Hughes

"Negroes - Sweet and docile, meek, humble, and kind: Beware the day they change their minds." - Langston Hughes

"Blame me for the outcome, ban my records. Check it! Don't have to bump this but please respect it!" - Tupac Shakur

"I believe in the brotherhood of all men, but I don't believe in wasting brotherhood on anyone who doesn't want to practice it with me. Brotherhood is a two-way street." - Malcolm X

"Nonviolence is fine, as long as it works." - Malcolm X

"Men ought either to be indulged or utterly destroyed, for if you merely offend them, they take vengeance, but if you injure them greatly, they are unable to retaliate, so that the injury done to a man ought to be such that vengeance cannot be feared." - Niccolo Machiavelli

"When it's time to die, be a man and pick the way you leave." - Tupac Shakur

"I have decided to stick with love. Hate is too great a burden to bear." - Rev. Dr. Martin Luther King, Jr.

"Be peaceful, be courteous, obey the law, respect everyone, but if someone puts his hand on you, send him to the cemetery." - Malcolm X

"I don't even call it violence when it is self-defense; I call it intelligence." - Malcolm X

"To the homies that I used to have that no longer roll, catch a brother at the crossroads." - Tupac Shakur

"Before I think computer chips, I gotta deal with brothers flipping. I don't see no devils breathing, only black blood dripping. We can change!" - Tupac Shakur

"Hence it comes about that all armed prophets have been victorious, and all unarmed prophets have been destroyed. Before all else, be armed." - Machiavelli

"I can resist everything except temptation." - Oscar Wilde

"For the sin they do by two and two they must pay for one by one." - Rudyard Kipling

"It ain't no sin if you crack a few laws now and then, just so long as you don't break any."
- Mae West

"He that falls into sin is a man, that grieves at it, is a saint, that boasteth of it, is a devil." - Thomas Fuller

"Sin is first pleasing, then it grows easy, then delightful, then frequent, then habitual, then confirmed, then the man is impenitent, then he is obstinate, then he is resolved never to repent, and then he is ruined." - Robert Leighton

"If a man, holding a belief which he was taught in childhood or persuaded of afterwards, keeps down and pushes away any doubts which arise about it in his mind, purposely avoids the reading of books and the company of men that call into question or discuss it, and regards as impious those questions which cannot easily be asked without disturbing it, the life of that man is one long sin against mankind." - W.K. Clifford

"What that fuck is you really complaining about? I know niggas that's never gonna make it out. This that shit you won't see in the media. Poor get poorer and the rich get greedier. Lot of daddies going back and forth out of jail, lots of sons growing up and repeating them. This is the belly of the beast; you won't make it out. Man, this shit was designed to just eat us up and my momma told me "nigga if you keep it up, you gone end up in prison just sweepin' up. Remember nobody never believed in us, when they see us now, they can't believe it's us." - Meek Mill

"I am a man more sinn'd against than sinning." - William Shakespeare

"Let these words be the last to my unborn seeds, help me raise my young nation in this world of greed. Currency means nothing if you still ain't free, money breeds jealousy, take the game from me." - Tupac Shakur

"Of mankind we may say in general they are fickle, hypocritical, and greedy of gain." - Machiavelli

"America will never be destroyed from the outside. If we lose our freedoms, it will be because we have destroyed ourselves from within." - Abraham Lincoln

"You claim I'm selling crack, but you be doing that. I'd rather say see ya, cause I would never be ya. Be an officer? You wicked overseer. You hotshot, wanna get props and be a savior. First, show a little respect, change your behavior, change your attitude, change your plan. There could never really be justice on stolen land." - KRS-One

"This ain't entertainment, it's for niggas on the slave ship. These songs just the spirituals that I swam against them waves with. Ended up on shore to their amazement, now I hope the example I set is not contagious. Lock us behind gates but can't tame us. Used to be 'Stay safe,' now it's 'Stay dangerous.' - Nipsey Hussle

"The only way for me to come back is like Makaveli. That's me. All these motherfuckers stole from me. I'm taking back what's mine." - Tupac Shakur

Time Period Reference Photos

A LETTER FROM HUEY TO THE REVOLUTIONARY BROTHERS AND SISTERS ABOUT THE WOMEN'S LIBERATION AND GAY LIBERATION MOVEMENTS

During the past few years, strong movements have developed among women and among homosexuals seeking their liberation. There has been some uncertainty about how to relate to these movements.

Whatever your personal opinions and your insecurities about homosexuality and the various liberation movements among homosexuals and women (and I speak of the homosexuals and women as oppressed groups), we should try to unite with them in a revolutionary fashion. I say "whatever your insecurities are" because, as we very well know sometimes our first instinct is to want to hit a homosexual in the mouth and want a woman to be quiet. We want to hit the homosexual in the mouth because we're afraid we might be homosexual; and we want to hit the woman or shut her up because we're afraid that she might castrate us, or take the nuts that we might not have to start with.

We must gain security in ourselves and therefore have respect and feelings for all oppressed people. We must not use the racist type attitude like the White racists use against people because they are Black and poor. Many times the poorest White person is the most racist, because he's afraid that he might lose something, or discover something that he doesn't have; you're some kind of threat to him. This kind of psychology is in operation when we view oppressed people and we're angry with them because of their particular kind of behavior, or their particular kind of deviation from the established norm.

Remember, we haven't established a revolutionary value system; we're only in the process of establishing it. I don't remember us ever constituting any value that said that a revolutionary must say offensive things towards homosexuals, or that a revolutionary should make sure that women do not speak out about their own particular kind of oppression. Matter of fact it's just the opposite: we say that we recognize the women's right to be free. We haven't said much about the homosexual at all, and we must relate to the homosexual movement because it's a real thing. And I know through reading and through my life experience, my observations, that homosexuals are not given freedom and liberty by anyone in the society. Maybe they might be the most oppressed people in the society.

And what made them homosexual? Perhaps it's a whole phenomena that I don't understand entirely. Some people say that it's the decadence of capitalism. I don't know whether this is the case; I rather doubt it. But whatever the case is, we know that homosexuality is a fact that exists, and we must understand it in its purest form: That is, a person should have freedom to use his body in whatever way he wants to. That's not endorsing things in homosexuality that we wouldn't view as revolutionary. But there's nothing to say that a homosexual cannot also be a revolutionary.

SUPREME COMMANDER, BLACK PANTHER PARTY

And maybe I'm now injecting some of my prejudice by saying that "even a homosexual can be a revolutionary." Quite on the contrary, maybe a homosexual could be the most revolutionary.

When we have revolutionary conferences, rallies and demonstrations there should be full participation of the gay liberation movement and the women's liberation movement. Some groups might be more revolutionary than others. We shouldn't use the actions of a few to say that they're all reactionary or counterrevolutionary, because they're not.

We should deal with the factions just as we deal with any other group or party that claims to be revolutionary. We should try to judge somehow, whether they're operating sincerely, in a revolutionary fashion, from a really oppressed situation. (And we'll grant that if they're women, they're probably oppressed.) If they do things that are un-revolutionary or counter-revo-

lutionary, then criticize that action. If we feel that the group in spirit means to be revolutionary in practice, but they make mistakes in interpretation of the revolutionary philosophy, or they don't understand the dialectics of the social forces in operation, we should criticize that and not criticize them because they're women trying to be free. And the same is true for homosexuals. We should never say a whole movement is dishonest, when in fact they're trying to be honest, they're just making honest mistakes. Friends are allowed to make mistakes. The enemy is not allowed to make mistakes because his whole existence is a mistake, and we suffer from it. But the womens liberation front and gay liberation front are our friends, they are potential allies, and we need as many allies as possible.

We should be willing to discuss the insecurities that many people have about homosexuality. When I say "insecurities", I mean the fear that they're some kind of threat to our manhood. I can understand this fear. Because of the long conditioning process which builds insecurity in the American male, homosexuality might produce certain hangups in us. I have hangups myself about male homosexuality. Where, on the other hand, I have no hangup about female homosexuality. And that's phenomena in itself. I think it's probably because male homosexuality is a threat to me, maybe and the females are no threat.

We should be careful about using those terms that might turn our friends off. The terms "faggot" and "punk" should be deleted from our vocabulary, and especially we should not attach names normally designed for homosexuals to men who are enemies of the people, such as Nixon or Mitchell. Homosexuals are not enemies of the people.

We should try to form a working coalition with the Gay liberation and Women's liberation groups. We must always handle social forces in the most appropriate manner. And this is really a significant part of the population both women, and the growing number of homosexuals that we have to deal with.

ALL POWER TO THE PEOPLE!

Huey P. Newton,
SUPREME COMMANDER,
Black Panther Party

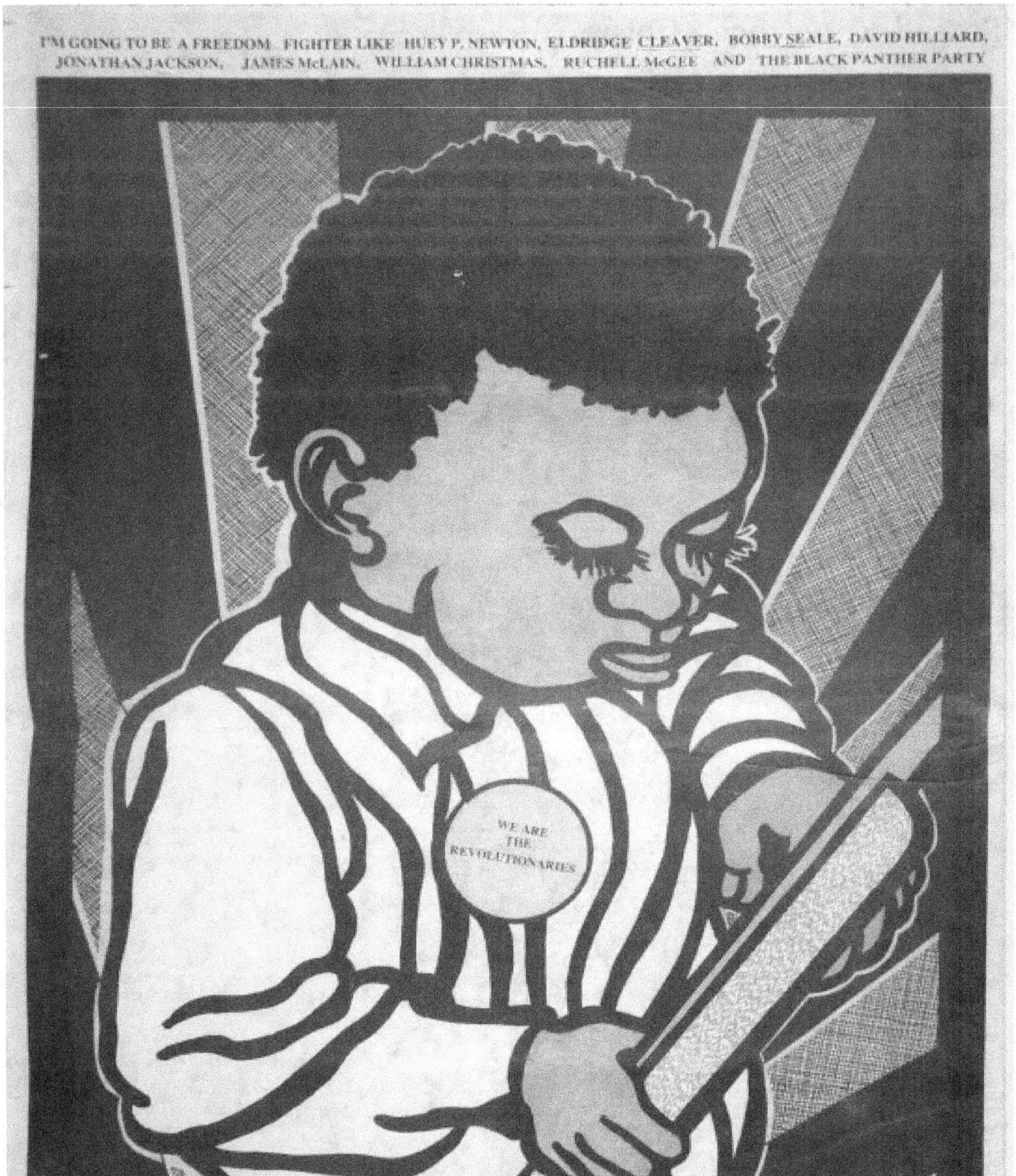
I'M GOING TO BE A FREEDOM FIGHTER LIKE HUEY P. NEWTON, ELDRIDGE CLEAVER, BOBBY SEALE, DAVID HILLIARD, JONATHAN JACKSON, JAMES McLAIN, WILLIAM CHRISTMAS, RUCHELL McGEE AND THE BLACK PANTHER PARTY
WE ARE THE REVOLUTIONARIES
EMORY
THE YOUTH MAKE THE REVOLUTION

NIGGA

"Never Ignorant Getting Goals Accomplished"

What Does This Mean to You?

"Education is the passport to the future, for tomorrow belongs to those who prepare for today?" – Malcolm X

"My daddy Alabama, my mamma Louisiana. You mix that negro with that creole, make a Texas bamma. I like my heir with baby hair and afros. I like my negro nose with Jackson Five nostrils." – Beyonce Knowles

"Now a willpower that I have polished with an artist delight will sustain some shaky legs and some weary lungs. I will do it. Give a thought once in a while to this little soldier of fortune of the twentieth century." – Ernesto "Che" Guevara

"Tell the babies that I love them. Precious boys and girls, born black in this white man'z world." – Tupac Shakur

"You should fight to be among the best in school. The very best in every sense and you already know what that means, study and revolutionary attitude. In other words; good conduct, seriousness, love for revolution, comradeship. I was not that way at your age, but I lived in a different society, where man was an enemy of man. Now you have the privilege of living in another era, and you must be worthy of it." - Ernesto "Che" Guevara

"Find out how much God has given you and from it take what you need; the remainder is needed by others." – St. Augustine

"Can't reach the children cause they illin'. Addicted to killing and the appeal from the cap peeling. Without feeling, will they last or be blasted, hardheaded bastard maybe you'll listen in this casket. The aftermath!" – Tupac Shakur

"A man who has never gone to school may steal from a freight car; but if he has a university education, he may steal the whole railroad." – Theodore Roosevelt

"Do not interfere with an army that is returning home. When you surround an army, leave an outlet free. Do not press a desperate foe too hard." – Sun Tzu

"Change does not roll in on the wheels of inevitability but comes through continuous struggle. And so we must straighten our backs and work for our freedom. A man can't ride you unless your back is bent." – Rev. Dr. Martin Luther King, Jr.

My Block

Tupac Shakur, Better Days Disc II

(Intro)

Take a ride to my block

My block, that's right

Around my motherfuckin' block

They got a nigga sheddin' tears, reminiscing on my past years, 'cause shit was hectic for me last year. It appears that I been marked for death, my heartless breath. The underlying cause of my arrest, my life is stressed. And no rest, forever weary, my eyes stay teary for all the brothers that are buried in the cemetery. Shit is scary, how black on black crime legendary, but at times unnecessary. I'm getting worried. Teardrops and closed caskets, the 3-strike law is drastic, it's certain death for us ghetto bastards. What can we do when we're arrested, but open fire? Life in the pen ain't for me, 'cause I'd rather die. But don't cry through the despair, I wonder if the Lord still cares for us nigga's on welfare. And who cares if we survive, the only time they notice a nigga is when he's clutchin' on a 4 5. My neighborhood ain't the same, 'cause all the little babies gone crazy or they suffering in the game. And I swear it's like a trap, but I ain't giving up on the hood, it's all good when I go back. Hoes showing me love, niggas giving me props. Forever hot, 'cause it don't stop…on my block.

(Hook)

Living life is but a dream. Hard times is all we see, every block is kind of mean, but on

the block we still pray.

Now shit is constantly hot on my block, it never fails to hear gunshots. Can't explain a mother's pain when her son drops. Black males living in hell, when will we prevail? Fearing jail, but crack sales got me living well. In a sense it's suicidal, with this thug life. Staying strapped, forever trapped in this drug life. God help me cause I'm starving, can't get a job, so I resort to violent robbin' my life is hard. Can't sleep because all the dirt makes my heart hurt. Put in work and shed tears for my dead peers. Misled from a childhood where I went astray. Til this day I still pray for a better way. Can't help but feel helpless and heart broke. From the start I felt the racism 'cause I'm dark. Couldn't quit the bullshit, made me represent. Hit the bar, play the star everywhere I went. In my heart I felt alone, out here on my own. I close my eyes and picture home. On my block.

And I can't help but wonder why so many young kids had to die. Caught strays from AK's and the drive bys. Swollen pride and homicide don't coincide. Brothers cry for broken lives, momma come inside. 'Cause our block is filled with danger. Used to be a close-knit community, but now we all cold strangers. Time changes us to stone then crack pipes. All up and down the block exterminating black life. But I can't blame the dealers. My momma's welfare check has brought the next man chrome wheels. Shit's real, I know you feel my tragedy. A single mother with a problem child, daddy-free. Hangin' out and pickin' up game, sippin' cheap liquor. Gamin' all the hoochies hoping I can get to sleep with her. It's a man's world, staying strapped. Fantasies of a nigga livin' phat, but held back. Pipe dreams can make the night seem hopeless, wide-eyed I'm losing focus. On my block.

And block parties in the projects lasting way past daylight. A young nigga learned to break night. Used to play fight with my homies but they stuck in the pen. I send them ends, but it's tough on a friend. In my mind I see the same motherfuckers ballin'. Alcohol will make a lazy nigga slip and fall, miss his call. I know that young niggas understand this, growing up in this world where everything is scandalous. I reminisce on the fast times, past crimes. Trying to cop a slice of pizza with my last dime. Can't explain just what attracts me to this dirty game. Gold chains, some extra change and the street fame. And what's strange is everybody know my name swear they all know me. And lots of cash make a nigga change. I hit the green just to maintain. Feeling pain for all the niggas that I lost to the game, from my block.

RIP to all the motherfuckers who passed away. From all the blocks that I'm from. 112th street and 7th Ave. NY, Uptown. 183rd and Walt, my block, that's right 127 and Morningside, my block, that's right, Decatur Ave. Baltimore, my block. In the jungle, Marin City, that's my block LA, that's my block too. Oakland, can't forget Oaktown, that's my block for sure. And all the other blocks around this motherfucker. Houston, Florida, St. Louis, Tennessee, Miami, Chicago. All yall nigga's stay kickin' up dust. Stay representin' the motherfuckin' block!"

Let's Talk About it

Tupac wrote another heartfelt classic with this one. These lyrics are filled with emotion, compassion, despair, and hope. These words sum up the daily emotions regarding community, family and friendships that feel pride, heartache, disappointment, happiness, pain, and joy of the urban ghetto experiences over generations.

Tupac opens this song by asking his listeners to mentally take a drive through these impoverished hoods, the land of the lost and forgotten. Tupac states that he's "shedding tears, reminiscing on my past fears, 'cause life was hectic for me last year," and later he says, "my eyes stay teary for all the brothers that are buried in the cemetery, shit is scary, how black on black crime's legendary, but at times unnecessary."

Discussion

1. Tupac referred to shedding tears. Do you have a hard time imagining tough men crying? How do you feel when you see a man crying?
2. There are indeed childhood fears, but what are some fears that adults face?
3. What is your opinion on black-on-black crime? Do you think it's a choice?
4. Do other races harm one another? Why are these crimes not called out as much as black-on-black crime by the media and society?
5. Does black on black crime excuse the killing of black people by other means?

Tupac specifically states that black on black crime is "at times unnecessary." It seems that he is saying that at times, crime is necessary.

1. When would crime be necessary?
2. Has violence been glorified?
3. Is there a recurring theme of violent offenders in our TV programming?
4. What are your thoughts about "an eye for an eye"?

Tupac states, "the three strikes law is drastic and certain death for us ghetto bastards. What can we do when we're arrested but open fire? Life in the pen ain't for me 'cause I'd rather die." On November 4, 1994, led by California, Congress passed the Three Strikes Law. In short, this means once a person has been charged with their third felony, the penalty is an automatic 25 years to life sentence. A felony is a crime punishable by a year or more in prison.

Some who oppose the Three Strikes Law believe that consideration should be given to victimless crimes and argue that the law strips the application of subjective analysis by judges. Critics also call it one of the harshest sentencing schemes of the generation. The law was passed largely because of public reaction to a horrific crime committed against an 18-year-old young woman named Kimber Reynolds and against 12-year-old Polly Klaas, both by men with prior criminal offenses.

The felonies included crimes such as juvenile offenses and petty theft, like receiving stolen goods or possession of small amounts of drugs. There are cases in which people who have stolen small retail items or written fraudulent checks have received 25 years to life sentences because the crime was a third felony. In one well-known case, father-of-three Leandro Andrade is serving consecutive life sentences for shoplifting nine children videos on two occasions in 1995. One out of four prisoners in the California penal system was sentenced under the Three Strikes Law, thus making it responsible for the massive overcrowding and separation of families.

Supporters argue that the law deters repeat offenders with one or two felonies and aids in getting repeat offenders off the street. They would argue a better example of the people convicted under this law would be of a person who has received his second handgun charge who had previously served years for attempted murder.

Here is one example:

Court of Appeals for the Ninth Circuit

Filed: December 30th, 2008

Precedential Status: Precedential

Citations: 551 F.3d 875

Docket Number: 06-56523

Panel: Jay S. Bybee, William Cameron Canby Jr., Andrew Jay Kleinfeld

Judges: William C. Canby, Jr., Andrew J. Kleinfeld, and Jay S. Bybee, Circuit Judges

551 F.3d 875 (2008)

Cecilio GONZALEZ, Petitioner-Appellant,

v.

W.A. DUNCAN, Respondent-Appellee.

No. 06-56523.

United States Court of Appeals, Ninth Circuit.

Argued and Submitted April 9, 2008.

Filed December 30, 2008.

*876 Sean K. Kennedy, Federal Public Defender, Gia Kim (argued), Deputy Federal Public Defender, Los Angeles, CA, for the petitioner-appellant.

Edmund G. Brown, Jr., Attorney General of the State of California, Dane R. Gillette, Chief Assistant Attorney General, Pamela C. Hamanaka, Senior Assistant Attorney General, Kenneth C. Byrne, Supervising Deputy Attorney General, Carl N. Henry (argued), Deputy Attorney General, *877 Los Angeles, CA, for the respondent-appellee.

Before: WILLIAM C. CANBY, JR., ANDREW J. KLEINFELD, and JAY S. BYBEE, Circuit Judges.

BYBEE, Circuit Judge:

Cecilio Gonzalez was convicted by a jury of failing to update his annual sex offender registration within five working days of his birthday, in violation of California Penal Code § 290(a)(1)(D).[1] Because of his prior criminal convictions, he received a sentence of 28 years to life imprisonment under California's "Three Strikes" law. On habeas review, we must decide whether his sentence violates the Eighth Amendment's prohibition against cruel and unusual punishment and, if so, whether the contrary conclusion of the California Court of Appeal constituted an unreasonable application of clearly established federal law.

The case is quite lengthy and worth the time to read the framing of the arguments and ultimate decisions made or overturned.

1. What is your opinion of the Three Strikes Law?
2. Is it fair and balanced?

The Rockefeller law was first introduced in May 1973 by Governor Nelson Rockefeller; the popular law aimed to deter drug use and their sales by an extreme minimum 15 year to life prison sentence for offenders. At the time the criteria for conviction were the sale of at least 2 ounces or the possession of 4 ounces of a narcotic, typically heroin or cocaine. Eventually more judges and more prisons were needed, as people were being sentenced at an alarming rate.

In 1977, the law was adjusted to exclude marijuana under 7/8 of an ounce, at the same time causing an uproar amongst legal groups because it did not deter the use of drugs. The law was deemed a failure by many. In 1979, the amount of drugs needed to trigger the 15 years to life sentence was increased because the funding and legal resources required to enforce the law were prohibitive. Later in the mid-1980s during the rise of the crack era, the Rockefeller Law changed again and *decreased* the required amount of drugs to be sold or possessed for 15 years to life sentence.

Even those in possession of these low quantities were punished in this manner; treatment and rehabilitation programs were not options if the quantity requirement was met. In 2009, Governor David Paterson reformed Three Strikes and permitted judicial discretionary power, a major omission in previous versions. This now empowers judges to consider special circumstances for addicts and first or second offenders in comparison to major drug criminals who cause terrible, long-term harm to youth and vulnerable families.

Tupac goes on to tell us, "But don't cry through your despair, I wonder if the Lord still cares for us niggas on welfare. And who cares if we survive, the only time they notice a nigga is when he's clutchin' on a 4 5."

Consider the infrastructure of our poor neighborhoods, and the educational, healthcare, and judicial systems from county to county and state to state. How different are they from our more affluent neighborhoods. These systems appear unfair and unbalanced across all social classes, demonstrated by daily decisions about where your own kids can play, or what hospitals and school systems are preferred. Grocery shopping, exercise and other errands can also be subconsciously chosen by the class of the neighborhood.

People call these places home, but others subconsciously or consciously avoid them. They live there, they love there their goals in life are made there. The desire for safety and safe policing is just as important and necessary there as in an affluent community. Tupac is speaking for those that have reason to wonder if the powers that be care about their well-being at all and why it seems their communities only make the news if someone commits a crime. The roses that grew from this concrete aren't typically what is telegraphed in most news stories.

1. How can society demonstrate to the children growing up in these neighborhoods that it cares about the communities?

2. What are some things you can do to personally make a difference?

3. Do you believe that people who are a product of the ghetto and claim thug life can believe in God?

4. How do you know that your God loves you? Does God love the homeless man?

5. Does God love those that have endured suffering or tragedy?

We should all take a walk through the hallways of an inner-city school, sit inside a classroom, and check out the reading materials the students have to use, go to the restroom and actually use it. Visit a public health clinic or your local homeless shelter to really understand the major differences and the struggles that are among us. In order to feel compassion, we should allow ourselves the opportunity to be vulnerable to the uncomfortable awareness of what is going on in our impoverished neighborhoods.

Tupac goes on to say, "My neighborhood ain't the same, cause they all gone crazy or their suffering in the game. And I swear it's like a trap, but I ain't given up on the hood, it's all good when I go back." Think deeply about the word "suffering."

By definition, suffering means to undergo or endure pain or distress. Growing up in these forgotten and feared neighborhoods meets the definition. American-manufactured guns, numerous liquor licenses, and imported drugs have taken over, and the powers that have allowed it. This was not by accident; it is strongly believed that ghettos were made by design, a conscious effort to consolidate and limit the resources of poor people. Meanwhile, our youth is expected to somehow weed through all of this with the hope of not being caught up in its vicious cycle or "trap," as Tupac called it.

These low-income neighborhoods do not manufacture guns or control the docks and other channels where these drugs are being imported by the ton. Yet it comes into these areas in droves since the coming of the civil rights movement, which coincidently or not, is about the same time oppressed people began to feel empowered and the oppressors began to feel real push back. Children are not born into poverty by choice. A child whose mother is a whore, or a drug addict is not by choice. A fatherless child is not by choice. Abuse, neglect and a poor education and healthcare system is not by choice.

These urban generational cycles are pandemics with no boundaries. Its effect will spread into higher income neighborhoods, no matter your race or social class.

Frederick Douglass once said, "where justice is denied, where poverty is enforced, where ignorance prevails and where any one class is made to feel that society is an organized conspiracy to oppress, rob, and degrade them, neither man nor persons will be safe." Infamous oppressors know this; they have studied the words of Sun Tzu: "If your enemy is secure at all points, be prepared for him. If he is superior in strength, evade him. If your opponent is temperamental, seek to irritate him. Pretend to be weak, that he may grow arrogant. If he is taking his ease, give him no rest. If his forces are united, separate them. If sovereign and subject are in accord, put division between them. Attack him where he is unprepared, appear where you are not expected".

Are the geographic and logistical nature of our poorest communities an accident? Is the minority migration into these pre-chosen lands, followed by the infiltration of guns and drugs a coincidence?

Ronald Reagan's infamous war on drugs started when its damaging effects poured over into more affluent communities. Prior to then, in the ghetto killer drugs like crack were used openly in the street and in broad daylight.

History has proven when the powers that be become fearful of an uprising, the oppressors take extreme measures to maintain order. The KKK was originally founded in Tennessee in 1866 as a decentralized social group that opposed the government's Reconstruction Act, sponsored in Congress by the Republican Party. At this time, the KKK opposed government intervention and its desire to bring them back into the Union. These citizens wanted to maintain their independence and did not want to fall under the rule and legislation of this America post-Civil War and by default, slavery.

It is taught that the Civil War's purpose was to abolish slavery, and this is simply not true. The Civil War which lasted from 1861 to 1865 was a war on politics and economics. In July 1861, Congress passed a resolution which declared that the war is being fought to protect the Union, and not to destroy slavery. While Lincoln's platform during his run for the presidency in 1860 did denounce slavery, it was after this election that Southern states began to secede from the Union beginning with South Carolina, followed by other Southern states; forming the Confederate States.

In February 1861, the Confederate States were formed under West Point Graduate and a United States Army Officer, Jefferson Davis who served as president of the Confederacy. The following month, Lincoln was sworn in as the President of the United States.

The Civil War began thereafter. In short, the KKK became a presence post-Civil War, a century earlier than most are aware of. Intervention by newly formed congressional laws and the federal government halted the Klan's rise and it died out between 1871 and 1872. The Klan's second rise to power in 1915 was during World War I due to the effects of the Great Depression. The third phase, the most organized and deadly, was in the 1960's to enforce Jim Crow laws and to combat the rise of the black and brown fight for equality also known as the Civil Rights Movement. The KKK used harsh tactics such as hangings, dismemberment, torture, deadly beatings and perhaps worst of all, local law enforcement and the judicial system, to instill fear and discipline in black America.

The CoinTelPro (counterintelligence program), secretly developed by the FBI, was used throughout the generations to infiltrate activist groups around the globe. It became painfully illegal and blatantly criminal during the Civil Rights Movement at the rise of popular and powerful activist groups such as The Black Panther Party (BPP). Its lawless power and influence rose as high up in the ranks as J. Edgar Hoover, CIA Director. J. Edgar Hoover had written, in a now declassified government document, "The Breakfast for Children Program represents the best and most influential activity going for the BPP and, as such, is potentially the greatest threat to the efforts by authorities to neutralize the BPP and destroy what it stands for".

The CoinTelPro had the ability to halt grass root organizations in their tracks through intimidation, manipulation, infiltration, malicious planting of false evidence, lies, deceit and murder. Once this program came to light by the media and the public, Congress disbanded its abuse of the secret intelligence and enacted laws to prevent the misuse in 1971. Tupac refers to his neighborhood as being like a trap when he says, "and I swear it's like a trap, but I ain't giving up on the hood, it's all good when I go back".

1. How do you think these poor neighborhoods, also referred to as ghettos, were created?
2. How do low wages, unlimited guns, liquor stores, poor education and health end up in minority neighborhoods, but not in the more affluent ones like Orange County in CA to Bergen County in NJ?
3. Hurricane Katrina destroyed the Lower 9th Ward and surrounding low-income communities. Affluent areas such as Main St. primarily went unharmed. Do you believe that was a result of poor infrastructure or human intervention?
4. Should the KKK be recognized as a social organization or as a hate group? What about Black Lives Matter? Proud Boys?
5. What is your understanding of the purpose of the Civil War?
6. What are some pros and cons of these government and monitoring programs such as the FBI's CoinTelPro or the Patriot Act?

The chorus in this piece is of children singing "Living life is but a dream, hard times is all we see, every block is kind of mean, but on the block we still pray. But on the block we still pray." Churches are prevalent in urban communities, perhaps because historically churches have been the primary source of strength and stability during dark times.

The black church has helped generations of communities bear the burden of hundreds of years of mistreatment, racism, and classism. It encouraged forgiveness and to let go of the anger born out of African American ancestors suffering here in America, due to the theft of endless labor, African names and religion, the destruction of ancient African genius of science, farming, medicine and astronomy, the selling off of their children, mothers and fathers, sisters and brothers at slave auctions, and even inventions. This has all significantly contributed to making many nations very wealthy.

Africans were shipped across oceans to build many nations, not just the United States, and have made those nations great wealth too. Inner city churches seem to teach more on the Laws of Moses, and the Children of Israel in the Old Testament rather than the Life of David, Joshua, Peter and John in The New Testament. Many Hebrew Africans regard the Old Testament as African ancestral history. No matter your personal reference, these Saints of the bible suffered and remained faithful to God or found God after a sin-filled life and became dedicated and loyal servants of God. Tupac says, "but on the block we still pray."

1. Do you believe in the power of prayer?
2. What does prayer mean to you?
3. Have you remained prayerful during hard times?
4. Have you taught your children or the youth in your life how to pray or have a conversation with God?
5. Did the slavery of Africans take place here in America?
6. Should this part of America's history be taught today in our schools?
7. Should there be sensitivity training for Law Enforcement and The Military?
8. What other races were enslaved for generations at the hands of a ruling party?
9. Do you believe God allowed slavery? Or ended it?

Tupac goes on to write "Now shit is constantly hot on my block, it never fails to hear gun shots. Can't explain a mother's pain when her son drops." This is a powerful and breathtaking statement.

1. Can you speak of a mother that has buried her son due to senseless violence?

2. Why do you think Tupac did not mention a father's pain in dealing with the murder of a child?

3. Tupac is speaking of murder, but is he praising it or reporting it?

4. Is a reporter in Iraq, Libya or North Korea glorifying war and other inhumane practices or just reporting on it?

Tupac continues in this piece with "In a sense, it's suicidal, with this thug life. Staying strapped, forever trapped in this drug life. God help me, cause I'm starving, can't get a job, so I resort to violent robbings, my life is hard. Can't sleep cause all the dirt makes my heart hurt. Put in work and shed tears for my dead peers."

Tupac has been accused of glorifying gang life or violence through his music and his image. It seems, however, Tupac constantly warns society of the dangers of ignoring the pleas of our youth, the burdens of the ghetto. Tupac compares this violent lifestyle to suicide.

1. Were you aware, before reading this piece from Tupac that he compared living a violent life to suicide?

2. If living a violent life is suicidal, why do so many of our youth turn to it?

3. Can you imagine being so hungry that you become violent?

4. Have you ever considered the personal history of the person that appears to have chosen a life of crime and or drugs?

5. Do you believe this type of person lives with regrets? Do you believe God loves them?

6. Do you feel in all instances it is a choice? In what scenario can you imagine it not being a choice?

7. What can a person with negative background checks do for a living?

8. Is the penal system designed to rehabilitate?

9. Would you hire a convicted criminal?

In Tupac's next line he states, "misled from childhood where I went astray. 'Til this day, I still pray for a better way. Can't help but feel hopeless and heart broke. From the start I felt the racism because I'm dark. Couldn't quit the bullshit, made me represent. Hit the bar, played the star everywhere I went. In my heart I felt alone out here on my own. I close my eyes and picture home."

1. What are examples of a child going astray?
2. Who or what could have that type of impact on a child?
3. Tupac is no doubt of dark skin. Can darker skin tone contribute to increased negative racial experiences?
4. Does skin tone matter to you?
5. What are the skin tones of your five closest friends? Why do you think that is?
6. How do you handle stress?
7. Is support for mental health important?

Tupac, as an embedded journalist, reported on the events in the ghetto as he saw them, validating and confirming their existence. Major news channels do the same. In the journalistic world this certifies objectivity, credibility, and truth. In rap, it is as interpreted as glorification, membership, or a badge of honor.

1. What is the difference?
2. Is Tupac promoting the impoverished lifestyle of ghetto living or is he speaking of the mere fact that it exists here in America and other countries?
3. Is a reporter in Iraq, Vietnam or North Korea promoting the war and other inhumane acts or simply reporting on it?

The third verse in this piece Tupac speaks of the young children that are the real victims. "Swollen pride and homicide don't coincide" and its battle for power is killing our youth. Pride is one of the seven deadly sins. The other six are Envy, Anger, Sloth, Greed, Gluttony and Lust. The origin of defining these sins dates back to the days of 4th century Egypt and has transformed over the years, being altered in the sixth century by Pope Gregory the Great and tweaked by historians and churches to follow.

There was a lot of attention paid to these sins, because there needed to be a communicable understanding of what leads to human transgressions in a way that could be taught and understood amongst the masses. Our human sinful behavior needed a definition, and for centuries our religious and philosophical leaders have narrowed it down to these seven deadly sins.

Tupac intertwines these sins in his lyrics not because he himself is a sinner, but because we all fall short of perfection. He is speaking to people that most of us may never relate too. He touches all corners of the sane and insane that only a sinful, saintly, genius has the real ability to accomplish.

1. If you had to pick a sin that you feel you most struggle with, what would it be?
2. If the same question is asked of your peers about you, what would they say the sin you struggle with is?
3. When a community works together by way of family and economics, it inherently empowers itself, but if a community does not, in what other ways can a community still grow?
4. Stone is "the hard solid, nonmetallic mineral in which rock is made." Tupac says time changes us to stone. What does he mean?
5. If these stones were your neighbors, how do you survive? How would you prevent becoming a stone yourself? Would you really know the difference?

Tupac has an ability to weave himself into his lyrics so that the listener doesn't feel alone or ostracized. Finally, a person publicly communicates a concern for those struggling with thoughts of suicide, anger, and hopelessness.

When Tupac says "but I can't blame the dealers. My momma's welfare check has brought the next man chrome wheels. Shit's real, I know you feel my tragedy, a single mother with a problem child, daddy free." Tupac is not only speaking of his own upbringing but to hundreds of thousands of people out there just like him, of all colors, and across all continents. Dealers and addicts are colorless, classless, and ageless.

Tupac stated in the DVD *Tupac Vs.* something to the effect that until he has a plan for these dealers and gangbangers to get out of the ghetto, it's hard to knock them for what they do for survival in the ghetto.

Every person has a past, and an upbringing that contributes to who and what they are to our community. It is easy to blame the drug dealers for bringing harm and chaos to our neighborhoods. Consider the manufacturing and transportation industry that is allowing drugs and guns to come into these neighborhoods and be manufactured in this country. It can also be said that these drug cartels and gun manufacturers would not be as powerful if it were not for the demand for drugs and guns here in America. It's simply the law of supply and demand - Economics 101.

1. How effective are we in controlling the flow of illegal drugs and guns?
2. How effective are the DEA and ATF? Or the CIA?
3. Can you relate to being raised by drug addicted parents?
4. Does this child have the same opportunities as the child born into a home without addiction?
5. What are some of the damaging effects to this child? Short and long term?
6. Can a single woman raise a man? What are some of the pros and cons?
7. Can a single man raise a woman? What are some of the pros and cons?
8. What are some negative effects of either parent not living in the home?
9. What type of parent do you think that child will grow up to be?
10. How important is family to you?

Tupac goes on to say "fantasies of nigga livin' phat but held back. Pipe dreams can make the night seem hopeless, wide eyed I'm losing focus." Every single child has dreams and vast imaginations, whether it comes to fruition or not. The manner in which one follow those dreams are determined by many things.

1. If you were born into a home rattled with poverty, drug addition, child abuse, failing school systems, and police brutality, how would you fulfill your dreams? What might be your options?
2. What does a child born into these conditions see, hear, or learn?
3. What does a child born into these conditions become?
4. Should a portion of your taxes go towards programs such as education and housing that will improve these conditions?

Tupac closes this masterpiece by reminding us all that there can be joy in pain, with his reference to block parties and the hook of this song which signifies a community's free spirit and camaraderie. He has mastered, through lyrical melody, a ghetto story that has a beginning, middle, and end. People that have the desire to understand other walks of life should first be aware of their existence, care about it, and learn about it, all with an open mind and heart.

Tupac says, "Growing up in the world where everything is scandalous." This may be the toughest part of parenting today. This song was written pre-1996; the world of our youth was scandalous then, but more than 25 years later, the world can be even more so. The most disciplined and attentive parents are struggling with keeping this world from swallowing our children alive, no matter the class, wealth, nor the geographical environment.

The internet, TV, and radio have influence and unlimited access to our children. "Bitch" is allowed on prime-time TV and social media sites such as google and twitter both carry triple X porn videos for anyone to access.

1. Tupac's reference to maintaining a friendship with an inmate is tough on a friend. What "friend" is he referring to? The inmate serving time or the friend that is free with the obligation to support the friend in jail?

2. What does his "miss his call" mean to you in relation to alcohol and drug abuse?

3. By definition, scandalous means "offensive to propriety or morality." What part, if any, do you find of today's world to be scandalous?

4. How can a child grow up, without major flaws in a community where "everything is scandalous"?

5. Is it the FCC's responsibility to restrict what is in the media or is it the adults responsibility to limit and block access?

6. If you were born without, could "gold chains," quick cash, and popularity attract you?

7. Do you think you know your favorite celebrity?

In the end of the last verse Tupac sends peaceful and encouraging words of thanks to his homies past and present that are products of "the block." These block children's voices are the chorus and the subjects of this song. These children do grow up and they become our neighbors, the parents of our own children's friends, our own friends, and even coworkers.

1. Are you affected by the youth's lives of today?

2. Do you feel any responsibility for them?

Time Period Reference Photos

Members of the Philadelphia Chapter of the BPP were forced to strip naked after Philadelphia police and FBI agents raided the chapter office on August 30, 1970. The raid took place a week before the Revolutionary People's Constitutional Convention Plenary Session, which was held in Philadelphia and was a deliberate effort to sabotage the convention

1970 F.B.I. MEMO URGED "SPECIAL OPERATION" AGAINST B.P.P.

"RIDICULE, DISCREDIT, PROMOTE FACTIONALISM IN BLACK PANTHER PARTY"

"... Through this lawsuit we intend to bring an end to a long national nightmare, exposing that the most extreme and violent actions were employed by high government officials against citizens of this nation ... The full extent of the federal police extermination program against the Black Panther Party will completely horrify many Americans."

—Black Panther Party Statement
On Filing Its Lawsuit Against
The U.S. Government
December 1, 1976

Of the 295 "Black Nationalist" COINTELPRO actions that took place between 1967 and 1971, 233 were directed against the Black Panther Party. As the following 1970 FBI document reveals, the Bureau used its most vicious tactics in the "disruptive-disinformation operation" against the BPP

5/11/70

SAC, San Francisco

Director, FBI
COUNTERINTELLIGENCE AND SPECIAL OPERATIONS (RESEARCH SECTION)

The Bureau would like to offer for your consideration a proposal for a disruptive-disinformation operation targeted against the national office of the Black Panther Party (BPP). This proposal is not intended to be all inclusive or binding in any of its various phases, but only as a guide for the suggested action. You are encouraged to submit recommendations relating to revisions or innovations of the proposal.

1. The operation would be effected through close coordination on a high level with the Oakland or San Francisco Police Department.

2. Xerox copies of true documents, documents subtly incorporating false information, and entirely fabricated documents would be periodically anonymously mailed to the residence of a key Panther leader. These documents would be on the stationery and in the form used by the police department or by the FBI in disseminating information to the police. FBI documents, when used, would contain police routing or date received notations clearly indicating they had been pilfered from police files.

CONTINUED ON PAGE 54

COINTELPRO— "Disrupt, Misdirect, Neutralize" Black Liberation Struggle

"...the chief investigative branch of the federal government (FBI), which was charged by law with investigating crimes and preventing criminal conduct, itself engaged in lawless tactics and responded to deep-seated social problems by fomenting violence and unrest."

—Final Report
Senate Intelligence Committee
April 23, 1976

On March 7, 1974, seven secret memoranda detailing FBI plans to "disrupt, misdirect, discredit or otherwise neutralize" Black militant organizations were released to NBC newsman Carl Stern, who had sued the Justice Department for them under the Freedom of Information Act.

The memoranda, though heavily censored, exposed the Bureau's ruthless Counterintelligence Program to destroy the Black liberation struggle in America. Below, we reprint an August, 1967 memo authorizing the initiation of COINTELPRO actions against Black organizations. Although the memo was written 13 years ago, the actions it calls for are still being carried out today against Black and other Americans who dare to organize for change.

August 25, 1967
PERSONAL ATTENTION TO ALL OFFICES

CONTINUED ON PAGE 13

THE U.S. GOVERNMENT MURDERED THESE PEOPLE BECAUSE THEY WERE MEMBERS OF THE BLACK PANTHER PARTY

"CRIPPLING" OF BLACK PANTHER NEWSPAPER PLOTTED

"HINDER VICIOUS PROPAGANDA SPREAD BY B.P.P."

In May, 1970, FBI headquarters in Washington, D.C., at the direction of then Bureau director, J. Edgar Hoover, ordered its Chicago, Los Angeles, Miami, Newark, New Haven, New York, San Diego and San Francisco field offices to submit proposals for "crippling" THE BLACK PANTHER newspaper, the official publication of the Black Panther Party.

According to the memo sent out from FBI headquarters across the nation:

"The Black Panther Party newspaper is one of the most effective propaganda operations of the BPP.

"Distribution of this newspaper is increasing at a regular rate thereby influencing a greater number of individuals in the United States along the black extremist lines.

"Each recipient submit by 6/5/70 proposed counterintelligence measures which will hinder the vicious propaganda being spread by the BPP. The BPP newspaper . . . is the voice of the BPP and if it could be effectively hindered it would result in helping to cripple the BPP."

The Senate Intelligence Committee, in its final report issued in April, 1976, contained details of COINTELPRO activities to sabotage THE BLACK PANTHER newspaper. Contained in the report were excerpts from numerous FBI documents. Below, we present some of these excerpts, which point out the U.S. government's illegal efforts to muzzle Black Panther Party views.

". . . a vigorous inquiry by the Internal Revenue Service to have 'The Black Panther' report their income from the sale of over 100,000 papers each [is recommended]. Perhaps the Bureau through liaison at SOG [seat of government] could suggest such a course of action. It is noted that Internal Revenue Service at San Francisco is receiving copies of Black Panther Party funds and letterhead memoranda.

"It is requested that the Bureau give consideration to discussion with Internal Revenue Service requesting financial . . .

BPP members look over soaked BLACK PANTHER newspapers after an arson fire at paper's San Francisco distribution center in January, 1970. SAMUEL NAPIER (far right and standing at left in photo above), the national circulation manager of the paper, was assassinated on April 17, 1971, as part of the COINTELPRO plot to "cripple" the Party's paper.

agent in powdered form and when applied to a particular surface emits an extremely noxious odor rendering the premises surrounding the point of application uninhabitable. Utilization of such a chemical of course, would be dependent upon whether an entry could be achieved into the area which is utilized for the production of 'The Black Panther.'"

—San Diego Field Office
May 26, 1970 memorandum

This same memo continued to say:

"Another possibility which the Bureau may wish to consider would be the composition and mailing of numerous letters to BPP Headquarters from various points throughout the country on stationary [sic] containing the national emblem of the Minutemen organization. These letters in several different forms, would all have the common theme of warning the Black Panthers to cease publication or drastic measures would be taken by the Minutemen organization.

"Utilization of the Minutemen organization through direction of informants within that group would also be a very effective measure for the disruption of the publication of this newspaper."

At one time, FBI agents contacted United Airlines officials and inquired about the rates being charged for transporting THE BLACK PANTHER. An FBI memorandum states that the BPP was being charged "the general rate" for printed materials, but that in the future it would be forced to pay the "full legal rate allowable for newspaper shipment."

The memo went on to say:

"Officials advise that increase means approximately a 40 per cent increase. Officials agree to determine consignee in San Francisco and from this determine consignees throughout the United States and impose full legal tariff. They believe the airlines are due the differences in freight tariffs as CONTINUED ON PAGE 14

F.B.I. Director: "B.P.P. Breakfast Program Is A Threat"

One of the earliest and most respected Survival Programs of the Black Panther Party was its Free Breakfast for Schoolchildren Program. At its peak, the Breakfast Program provided hot, nutritious food five days a week for thousands of Black and poor children across the country.

According to a May, 1969, memo sent by J. Edgar Hoover to more than two dozen FBI offices, the Free Breakfast Program "represents the best and most influential activity going for the BPP and as such is potentially the greatest threat to efforts by authorities to neutralize the BPP and destroy what it stands for."

Hoover wrote that the Free Breakfast Program ". . . has met with some success and has resulted in considerable favorable publicity for the Black Panther Party.

"The resulting publicity tends to portray the BPP in a favorable light . . . and obscure the violent nature of the group and its ultimate aim of insurrection."

Continuing, the memo said that Free Breakfast Programs "promote at least tacit support for the BPP among naive individuals, both Black and White, and, what is more distressing, providing the BPP with a ready audience composed of highly impressionable youth of tender ages which to propagate its message of hate and violence."

So successful was the Free Breakfast for Schoolchildren Program in pointing up the hunger and poverty of Black and poor people amidst the wealth of this country, that the federal government eventually established the National Free Breakfast and Lunch Program as a mandatory service in all public schools.

In one 1969 case documented by the Senate Intelligence Committee, the FBI office in San Diego sent an anonymous letter to the bishop of the San Diego CONTINUED ON PAGE 11

BPP Free Breakfast for Schoolchildren Program . . . a target of . . .

(Lyrics to)

Me Against the World

Tupac Shakur, Me Against the World

(Intro)

It's just me against the world. Nothing to lose, It's just me against the world.

I got nothing to lose, It's just me against the world.

Stuck in the game. Me against the world baby.

Can you picture my prophesy? Stress in the City, the cops is hot for me. The projects is full of bullets, the bodies is dropping, there ain't no stopping me. Constantly moving while making millions, witnessing killings, leaving dead bodies in abandoned buildings. Can't reach the children, cause they illin, addicted to killing and the appeal from the cap peelin'. Without feelings, but will they last or be blasted? Hardheaded bastard, maybe he'll listen in this casket, the aftermath. More bodies being buried, I am losing my homies in a hurry. They're relocating to the cemetery, got me worried, stressing my vision's blurried. The question is, will I live? No one in the world loves me, I am headed for danger, don't trust these strangers, put one in the chamber whenever I'm feeling this anger. Don't wanna make excuses cause this is how it is. What's the use, unless we shooting, no one notices the youth. It's just me against the world.

Could somebody help me? I'm out here all by myself. See ladies in stores, baby Capones livin' wealthy. Pictures of my birth on this earth is what I'm dreaming. Seeing daddy's semen, full of crooked demons, already crazy and screaming. I guess them nightmares as a child had me scared but left me prepared for a while. Is there another route for a crooked outlaw, veteran, a villain, a young thug who one day shall fall?

With all this extra stressing the question I wonder is after death, after my last breath, when will I finally get to rest? Through this suppression, they punish the people that's asking questions. And those that possess, steal from those without possessions. The message I stress, to make it stop, study your lessons, don't settle for less. Even the genius asks questions, be grateful for blessings, don't ever change, keep your essence. The power is in the people and the politics that we address. Always do your best, don't let the pressure make you panic, and when you get stranded, and things don't go the way you planned it. Dream of the riches, in a position of making a difference. Politicians and hypocrites, they don't wanna listen. If I'm insane, it's the fame that made a brother change. It wasn't nothing like the game. It's Just Me Against the World!

That's right. I know it seems hard sometimes but remember one thing. Through every dark night, there's a bright day after that. So no matter how hard it gets, stick your chest out, keep your head up and handle it.

Let's Talk About it

Tupac is in your face and unapologetic with this work. He clearly wants to be heard and to hold people accountable for today's youth in a system that seems to care for only profit and not a child's well-being. Prophecy by definition means prediction. Tupac asks if you can predict the outcome for a young child growing up where gangs, drugs and guns are present every day, where many fear neighbors and law enforcement.

Imagine a place where undisciplined children roam the playgrounds due to the absence of stable parenting or a homelife. A place where a child, who by the young age of 10 has seen more bad times than good that can damage a lifetime if not checked. In this song, Tupac appears to be frustrated with the state of our society and its impact on youth.

Tupac talked about writing this song during an interview from Dannemora Prison, where he served time for disorderly conduct. In the interview he talked about his forever love, children, expressing his disappointment that they suffer while society has written them off. Tupac understands doing that comes with consequences, hence his acronym Thug Life - The Hate You Give Little Infants Fucks Everyone. How does a child learn in an environment where their classrooms, books, food, and the ventilation systems are terrible? Some children make it to the twelfth grade with barely even an eighth grade reading level.

In this same song, Tupac speaks on the hypocrisy of the local preacher and politicians that pretend to care. Tupac said, "Politicians and hypocrites, they don't wanna listen."

1. Do Politicians that represent your community make appearances outside of the campaign trail?
2. What is your opinion on a Politicians level of honesty?
3. Do you feel responsibility for a child that is not your own?

Until the Voting Rights Act of 1965 was established, people of color were denied access to voting and often felt the effort was too dangerous or didn't matter. The act reinforced the right to vote under the Fifteenth Amendment which declares that all born citizens as well as former slaves have the right to vote, but these rights were still being denied on state and local levels.

Voting laws were made to create order and expectations. The goal was to develop and maintain class structures that were of power and of need. The strength of the black and brown vote had already proven its power and has been seen as a threat to the imbalance of power. In March 1867, just a few years after emancipation, black people voted in 22 members to Congress. Over the next century and more, individual states, counties and towns made it impossible for people of color to vote; over those years voting became to be viewed as a dangerous activity, enforced by law enforcement, and not worth the consequence, which was sometimes death. Judges critical to maintaining supremacy were put in place and laws were made that ensured generational long-term restrictions. Today we still see voter intimidation tactics, huge wealth discrepancies, the growth of the industrial penal system, police brutality, and unequal essential needs.

Discussion

1. Do you feel a responsibility for the lives and well-being of children who are not your own?

2. Can laws passed by politicians have a direct effect on our youth? How so?

3. With the laws you identified above, why would a law be enacted, or not, if our youth can be harmed by it? Who or what beneficiary of said law is worth this sacrifice?

4. Do you vote? Do your parents? Do you believe your vote or political party matters?

5. Do you believe in the American democratic system of fair and free elections?

6. Do you believe there should be criminal laws around voter intimidation?

7. What about voter fraud?

8. Should these laws be at a state or federal level? What are Pros and Cons?

Tupac goes on to say "can't reach the children, cause they illin, addicted to the killing and the appeal from the cap peelin'. Without feelings, but will they last or be blasted? Hardheaded bastard, maybe you'll listen in this casket, the aftermath." The words sound great poetically, but can and should we ignore the fact that these words are not just poetic but seem to be frighteningly real? Tupac is referring to a real element of our society and is it time to stop and understand how, why, and where we are responsible for this.

1. Can the youth Tupac is speaking of be reached?

2. Do you think the members of these gangs and supremacy gangs belong because they want to, or could it be because they feel they have to?

3. Is Tupac glorifying violence in this verse or is he denouncing it?

4. What policies do you support that directly support the poor and impoverished?

5. Have you ever felt that someone who is poor shouldn't own an iPhone or designer sneakers, or something else considered a high-end purchase?

6. Should organizations like the NRA help in improving the lives of our communities via safety measures such as a tracking or RFID technology for guns and bullets, free gun responsibility and awareness training, alcohol/ body temperature safety sensors?

7. Should the government enact more gun safety and control laws? What kinds would you support?

8. Should automatic weapons be available for civilian purchase?

This song continues on with "no one in the world loves me, I am headed for danger, don't trust these strangers, put one in the chamber whenever I'm feeling this anger. Don't wanna make excuses cause this is how it is. What's the use, unless we shooting, no one notices the youth. It's just me against the world." This is where Tupac seems very comfortable, in a place of simultaneous vulnerability and accountability, written in its most gangster form. His power to articulate is rare and comes along just once in a lifetime.

1. Have you ever felt unloved? How did it affect you? Why would someone feel that way?

2. What programs are available for the youth in your community? Are community social programs such as The Boys and Girls Club or afterschool programs necessary for children's development?

3. How do you handle anger? What is your greatest flaw while angry?

4. Do you feel a responsibility in keeping communities other than your own safe?

5. What does safe mean to you? What does safe mean to a child?

6. Have you ever had suicidal thoughts?

7. How would you handle a friend that speaks of suicide?

The closing verse to this song *Me Against the World* is possibly one of the best verses in Tupac's catalogue. It covers so many topics that have caused burdens and weariness amongst black and brown communities, and yet embraces the beauty and glory of the culture and potential as a people.

Tupac has diverse followers because he speaks to a wide range of people. He verbally attacks classism and systematic racism. He abhors the greedy, the liars, and the selfish. He warns us of these types in not just this song but in many in his catalogue.

He speaks on these societal traps that were once constructed for people of color and are now being used against other groups in our community. Police brutality is spreading outside of the once "only in black communities" to more suburban areas. Bad lands are now being approved for zoning in more affluent communities. Bad teachers are now teaching children in more affluent communities as well. A beast cannot be trained nor contained, if it is truly a beast. And this beast in the form of systematic oppression, is indeed a beast.

Tupac does not limit his audience in his verses. He speaks to us all. Imagine if this great orator was alive today. Would he have been able to move his audience to make changes so that society would look different now?

What Does This Mean to You II?

"Throw your soldiers into positions whence there is no escape, and they will prefer death to flight. If they will face death, there is nothing they may not achieve." - Sun Tzu

"We declare our right on this earth to be a human being, to be respected as human beings, to be given the rights as human beings in this society, on earth, in this day, which we intend to bring into existence by any means necessary." - Malcolm X

"Why does the guerilla fighter fight? We must come to the inevitable conclusion that the guerilla fighter is a social reformer, that he takes up in arms responding to the angry protest of the people against their oppressors, and that he fights in order to change the social system that keeps all his unarmed brothers in ignominy and misery." - Ernesto "Che" Guevara

"Usually when people are sad, they don't do anything. They just cry over their condition. But when they get angry, they bring about change." - Malcolm X

"Sitting by the Nile where the water flows, contemplating plots wondering where the thought will go. Brothers getting shot, coming back. Resurrect!" - Tupac Shakur

"I told you last album, we need help cause we dying. Give us a chance, help us advance cause we're trying. Ignore my whole plea watching us in discuss. Then you beg when my guns bust!" - Tupac Shakur

"Here is a message to the newborn waiting to breathe. If you believe then you can achieve. Just look at me." - Tupac Shakur

"Faith is taking the first step even when you don't see the whole staircase." - Rev. Dr. Martin Luther King, Jr.

"There is going to be some stuff that you are going to see that may make it hard to smile in the future. Through all the rain and the pain, you got to keep your sense of humor. You go to be able to smile through the bullshit." - Tupac Shakur

"Faith is to believe what you do not see; the reward of this faith is to see what you believe." - St. Augustine

"Every great dream begins with a dreamer. Always remember you have within you the strength, the patience, and the passion to reach for the stars to change the world." - Harriet Tubman

"Whosoever desires constant success must change his conduct with the times." - Machiavelli

"A return to first principles in a republic is sometimes caused by the simple virtues of one man. His good example has such an influence, that the good men strive to imitate him and the wicked are ashamed to lead life so contrary to his example." - Machiavelli

"God had one son on earth without sin, but never one without suffering." - Augustine of Hippo

"I love to see the block in peace. With no more dealers and crooked cops, the only way to stop the beast. And only we can change, it's up to us to clean up the streets it ain't the same. Too many funerals and too many tears, I just seen another brother buried plus I knew him for years." - Tupac Shakur

"Die when I may, I want it said of me by those who knew me best, that I always plucked a thistle and planted a flower where I thought a flower would grow." - Abraham Lincoln

"In three words I can sum up everything I have learned about life: It goes on." - Robert Frost

"God is not willing to do everything, and thus take away our free will and that share of glory which belongs to us." - Machiavelli

"Ima wade, Ima wade through the waters, 'til the tide don't move. Ima riot, Ima riot through your borders, call me bullet proof. Lord forgive me, I've been running. Running blind in truth. Ima wade, Ima wade through your shallow love. Tell the deep I'm new!" - Beyonce Knowles

"Do you wish to be great? Then begin by being. Do you desire to construct a vast and lofty fabric? Think first about the foundations of humanity. The higher your structure is to be, the deeper must be its foundation." - St. Augustine

"I close my eyes, because all I see is terror. I hate the man in the mirror because its reflection makes the pain turn realer." - Tupac Shakur

"I find, in being black, a thing of beauty: a joy, a strength, a secret cup of gladness, a native land in neither time nor space, a native land in every negro face! Be loyal to yourselves, your skin, your hair, your lips, your southern speech, your laughing, your kindness are Negro Kingdoms, vast as any other." - Ossie Davis

"This is the very imperfections of a man, to find out his own imperfections." - St. Augustine

"They called it the projects, they put us in projects. What they gonna do with us? Can't call the cops yet. You might just get popped at, cause they the ones shootin' us. I'm on my mom's steps, it's like a bomb threat. The violence pursuing us, I ain't meet God yet. Cause I'm on the block where it's just me and Lucifer, look what they do to us. They know we in poverty. When I went to court, the judge said, "Meek, you a menace to society." You said, you would give me a chance, your honor, why would you lie to me? 16 more years of probation, you know you gonna get more time on me. Whole hood goin' crazy, babies havin' babies. She was fourteen, actin' like she eighty. Got pregnant by a nigga, that was locked up in them cages. And the story goes on, if you make it, you amazing." - Meek Mill

"If I could have convinced more slaves that they were slaves, I could have freed more." - Harriet Tubman

"The future is still inside of me. We must remember that tomorrow comes after the dark. You will always be in my heart, with unconditional love." - Tupac Shakur

"If you have no confidence in self, you are twice defeated in the race called life." - Marcus Garvey

"When I held that nine, all I can see was my momma's eyes." - Tupac Shakur

"I see Bloods and Crips running up the hill, looking for a better way. My brothers and sisters, it's time to build cause even thug niggas pray." - Tupac Shakur

"So help me. Somebody save me. Lost and crazy. Scared to drop a seed, hoping I ain't cursed my babies." - Tupac Shakur

"It's sad because I bet Brenda doesn't even know. Just because you're from the ghetto doesn't mean you can't grow." - Tupac Shakur

"I see you trying to hide, hoping that nobody don't notice, you must always remember you still a member of the hopeless. See you're black like me and you snap like me, when these devils try to plot and trap our young black seeds." - Tupac Shakur

"Hold fast to dreams, for if dreams die, life is a broken winged bird that cannot fly. Hold fast to dreams, for when dreams go, life is a barren field. Frozen with snow." - Langston Hughes (Dreams)

"Being unwanted, unloved, uncared for, forgotten by everybody, I think that is a much greater hunger, a much greater poverty than the person who has nothing to eat." - Mother Teresa

"I am just one of the people sick of social order, sick of the establishment, sick to my soul of it all. To me, America's society is nothing but a cancer, and it must be exposed before it could be cured. I am not the doctor to cure it. All I can do is expose the sickness." - Nina Simone

"Every man must decide whether he will walk in the light of creative altruism or in the darkness of destructive selfishness." - Rev. Dr. Martin Luther King, Jr.

"Almost always, the creative dedicated minority has made the world better." - Rev. Dr. Martin Luther King, Jr.

"I grew up like a neglected weed – ignorant of liberty, having no experience of it." - Harriet Tubman

"God and nature first made us what we are, and then out of our own created genius we make ourselves what we want to be. Follow always the great law. Let the sky and God be our limit and eternity our measurement." - Marcus Garvey

"The great and glorious masterpiece of man is to know how to live with purpose." - Michel de Montaigne

"If we could only give, just once, the same amount of reflection to what we want to get out of life that we give to the question of what to do with a two weeks' vacation, we would be startled at our false standards and the aimless procession of our busy days." - Dorothy Canfield Fisher

"Our plans miscarry because they have no aim. When a man does not know what harbor he is making for, no wind is the right wind." - Marcus Annaeus Seneca

"Courage is the most important of all the virtues, because without courage you can't practice any other virtue consistently. You can practice any virtue erratically, but nothing consistently without courage."-Maya Angelou

"Out of the night that covers me. Black as the pit from pole to pole, I thank whatever Gods may be, for my unconquerable soul. In the fell clutch of circumstance, I have not winced nor cried aloud. Under the bludgeoning's of chance, my head is bloody, but unbowed. Beyond this place of wrath and tears, looms but the horror of the shade, and yet the menace of the years finds, and shall find me, unafraid. It matters not how straight the gate. How charged with punishments the scroll. I am the master of my fate. I am the captain of my soul." - William Ernest Henley (Invictus)

"There is no excuse for the young people not knowing who their heroes and heroines are or were." – Nina Simone

"How many legs does a dog have if you call the tail a leg? Four. Calling a tail a leg doesn't make it a leg." - Abraham Lincoln

Time Period Reference Photos

Panthers Ambushed--One Murdered

The Minister of Information, Eldridge Cleaver, is behind bars for life as a result of an attempted assassination on his life by the Oakland Police Department, the Gestapo strongarm of the racist power structure.

Eldridge Cleaver, Bobby Hutton, and eight other brothers were ambushed by the Oakland pigs on April 6, 1968... a set-up to put Eldridge Cleaver in prison for life and to wipe out the leadership of the Black Panther Party.

As a result, Bobby Hutton is dead, brutally murdered by a volley of pig bullets as he surrendered with his arms above his head.

The Minister of Information's parole was immediately revoked, and he is now imprisoned for three years, and faces life imprisonment on the charges stemming from the ambush. Cleaver was shot, has numerous buckshot wounds in his legs, was severely burned by tear gas on his chest and in his eyes, Police transported Cleaver from Oakland to Vacaville State Medical Facility "for security reasons" under machine gun guard, chained to a wheelchair, and heavily drugged.

Bail for Eldridge Cleaver was set at $63,000 even though it is strictly nonfunctional bail since his parole was immediately revoked, without trial, indictment, hearing, conviction, investigation, or any type of due process of law.

Cleaver and Hutton were forced to take refuge in a house located at 1218 28th Street, when police opened fire on them, at about 9:05 p.m., on the night of April 6, 1968.

Over four dozen pigs armed with OVERKILL weapons such as 351 magnums, 12 gauge shotguns, machine guns, stoner guns, and varied hand pistols carried on a 90 minute shootout with the victims who used a total of FIVE weapons, only two of which were rifles.

Although the pigs and the racist press repeatedly try to call the police ambush a Panther set-up, within two minutes after the police had stopped and pulled their weapons at 2906 Union Street, an entire two-block area was blocked off around Union, Magnolia, 28th and 30th Streets, and dozens of Emeryville and Oakland police officers had (supposedly answering a call for reinforcements) appeared on the scene thoroughly equipped with riot helmets, OVERKILL weapons, tear gas bombs... AND had notified the local racist press, who were on the spot as evidenced by their pictures and falsified radio reports from 10pm throughout the night.

The pigs fired off at least 1500 rounds of ammunition and shot numerous tear gas bombs into the residence to force Cleaver and Bobby Hutton out as well as randomly dangering the safety of other ghetto dwellers on the same block by firing aimlessly into their houses. When this tactic failed, the pigs and members of the Oakland Fire Department set fire to the house and forced the two to surrender.

Driven out by the burning flames and the stifling fumes of the tear gas, Bobby surrendered first, staggering out with his hands up - DEFENSELESS, UNARMED, OVERCOME BY FUMES — putting himself at the evil mercy of the pigs who waited until they recognized him and then gunned him down, killing him instantly and riddling his lifeless body with bullets.

The Minister of Information, who had had Hutton take off his clothes in the basement, to determine the extent of his wounds, came out stark naked, and was kicked by police officers, before being shoved into custody.

Now being held in jail on a charge of conspiracy to commit murder are six other brothers who were arrested by police the same night while in the area: David Hilliard, 25; Wendell Wade, 23; Terry Cotton, 21; Charles Bursey, 21, and Donnell Lankford, 18; bail is $40,000 for each of them. Warren Wells, 21, was shot in the buttocks during the action, and is also under a $40,000 bail. John L. Scott, 17, is still being detained at Juvenile Hall, under a $40,000 bail.

All of the above named are plaintiffs in a suit against the City of Oakland, and the Chief of Police of Oakland, which seeks to temporarily and permanently enjoin Coakley, the District Attorney, from criminal prosecutions of NEWTON, SEALE, CLEAVER, HUDSON, HILLIARD, CARTER, BURSEY, COTTON, LANKFORD, WAD, WELLS, AND STAFFORD.

o o o o o o o o o o

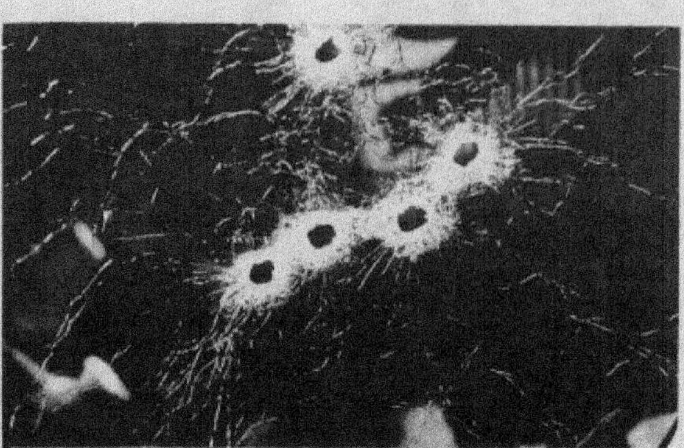

POLICE MURDERED A MAN, IMPRISONED A MAN, JAILED SEVEN OTHERS, RUINED THIS HOUSE AT 1218 - 28th ST, OAKLAND, AND SHOWED THE COUNTRY AND THE WORLD THE EXACT NATURE OF THE RACIST OPPRESION IN THE U.S.

STATEMENT

This statement was given by Eldridge Cleaver to Attorney Alex Hoffman at Vacaville on April 7 where Cleaver, Minister of Information of the Black Panther Party, was finally imprisoned in solitary confinement following the police murder of Bobby Hutton and wounding of Cleaver in Oakland on April 6:

"It is my opinion that this is the latest in a series of attempts to liquidate the leadership of the Black Panther Party by the Oakland Police Department.

"Already they have moved against Huey P. Newton, Minister of Defense, and they are well advanced in framing Bobby Seale, our Chairman. And now, for the first time, they have moved directly against me, shooting me, and attempting to kill me.

"I think that this is a calculated plan that is being carried out. △

EDITORIAL:

This is the second pig set-up to waste the leadership of the Black Panther Party. Six months ago, the Oakland Pig Department sent Officer Frank Frey and Officer Heanes to West Oakland to wipe out the Minister of Defense.

In the resulting shootout, Frey lost his life, the Minister of Defense was wounded, and later arraigned and indicted on a charge of murder and attempted murder.

The aim of the racist power structure is to stop the growing unity and awareness of the black community to the 400 year old systematic enslavement and oppression to which it has been subjected.

By killing our leaders and using Nazi gestapo tactics on the streets of the black communities from coast to coast, and harrassing black people in their homes, on their jobs, in the schools, on the streets, on the television, on the news, in books and in church, the

BOBBY/GARRY

Participants in the press conference pointed out that pictures and dossiers of Panther leaders have been distributed throughout California by the police along with description of the methods of dealing with them, that the entire pattern of the Oakland Police Department over a period of several months, predating October 28 when Newton was arrested on an alleged charge of murder, has been a concerted effort to harass and to kill and maim the militant leadership of the Black Panther Party.

On April 3, the police broke into a church where the Panthers were holding a meeting. The police came in with arms at the ready for action. Attorney for the Panther Party, Charles Garry, pointed out that even the Nazis did not have the audacity to break into places of worship. When the police broke into the church where the Panthers were meeting, he would not permit the sanctuary

REMEMBER THE WORDS OF BROTHER MALCOLM X

THE FOLLOWING STATE-
MENTS ARE EXERPTS
FROM MALCOLM'S SPEECH
"THE BALLOT OR THE
BULLET", GIVEN IN
CLEVELAND, APRIL 3,1964.

...I must say this con-
cerning the great controversy over rifles and shotguns.
the only thing that I've ever
said is that in areas where
the government has proven itself either unwilling or unable to defend the lives and
the property of Negroes, it's
time for Negroes to defend
themselves. Article number
twoof the constitutional
amendments provides you and
me the right to own a rifle
or a shotgun. It is constitu-
tionally legal to own a shotgun or a rifle. This doesn't
mean you're going to get a
rifle and form batalions and
go out looking for white
folks, although you'd be
within your rights - I mean
you'd be justified; but that
would be illegal. If the
white man doesn't want the
black man buying rifles and
shotguns, then let the government do its job. That's
all. And don't let the white
man come to you and ask you
what you think about what
Malcolm says - why, you old
Uncle Tom. He would never
ask you if he thought you
were going to say, "Amen!"
No, he is making a Tom out of
you.

So, this doesn't mean forming
rifle clubs and going out look-

Medals of Honor, with shoulders this wide, chests this
big, muscles that big- any
time you and I sit around and
read where they bomb a church
and murder in cold blood, not
some grownups, but four little
girls while they were praying
to the same god the white man
taught them to pray to, and
you and I see the government
go down and can't find who did
it.

Why, this man-he can find
Eichmann hiding down in Argen-

rifle clubs and going out looking for people, but it is time,
in 1964, if you are a man, to
let that man know. If he's not
going to do his job in running
the government and providing
you and me with the protection
that our taxes are supposed to
be for, since he spends all
those billions for his defense
budget, he certainly can't be-
grudge you and me spending $12
or $15 for a single-shot or
double-action. I hope you understand. Don't go out shooting
people, but any time, brothers
and sisters, and especially
the men in this audience-some
of you wearing Congressional

way, this same man that had
Eichmann hiding down in Argen-
tina somewhere. Let two or
three American soldiers, who
are minding somebody else's
business way over in South
Vietnam, get killed, and he'll
send battleships, sticking
his nose in their business. He
wanted to send troops down to
Cuba and make them have what
he calls free elections-this
old cracker who doesn't have
free elections in his own
country. No, if you ever see
me another time in your life,
if I die in the morning, I'll
die saying one thing: the
ballot or the bullet, the
ballot or the bullet.

Born May 19, 1925
Assinated Feb 21, 1965

OUTLAWS

"Operating Under Thug Law As Warriors"

What Does This Mean to You?

"A right delayed is a right denied." - Rev. Dr. Martin Luther King, Jr.

"Charity is no substitute for justice withheld." - St. Augustine

"Where justice is denied, where poverty is enforced, where ignorance prevails, and where any one class is made to feel that society is an organized conspiracy to oppress, rob, and degrade them, neither persons nor property will be safe." - Frederick Douglass

"Justice remains the tool of a few powerful interest; legal interpretations will continue to be made to suit the convenience of the oppressor powers." - Ernest "Che" Guevara

"We're all soldiers in God's eyes. Now it's time for war." - Tupac Shakur

"The change in consciousness will not take place automatically in the economy. The alterations are slow and are not harmonious; there are periods of acceleration, pauses and even retrogressions." - Ernesto "Che" Guevara

"If I choose to ride thuggin' until the day I die. Nobody gives a fuck about us! But when I start to rise a hero in their children's eyes, now they give a fuck about us!" - Tupac Shakur

"I'm seeing it clearer, hating the picture in the mirror. They claim we inferior, so why the fuck these devils fear us." - Tupac Shakur

"A man who is good enough to shed his blood for the country is good enough to be given a square deal afterwards." - Theodore Roosevelt

(Lyrics to)

Hail Mary

Makaveli, The Don Killuminati 7 Day Theory

Makaveli in this Killuminati all through your body. That blow is like a 12-gauge shotty. Feel me! And GOD said he shall send his one begotten son to leave the wild into the ways of the man. Follow me! He's my flesh, flesh of my flesh!
(Hook)
"Come with me. Hail Mary! Run quick see! What do we have here now? Do you wanna ride or die?"

I ain't a killer but don't push me! Revenge is like the sweetest joy next to getting pussy! Picture paragraphs unloaded, wise words being quoted, peeped the weakness in the rap game and sewed it. Bow down pray to God, hoping that he's listening. Seeing niggas comin' for me when my diamonds, when they glistening. Now pay attention, rest in peace Father. I am a ghost in these killing fields. Hail Mary catch me if I go. Let's go deep inside the solitary mind of a madman. Screams in the dark. Evil lurks, enemies, see me flee. Activate my hate! Let it break, til they blame me, set trip, empty out my clip, never stop to aim. Some say the game is all corrupted, fucked in this shit. Stuck niggas is lucky if we bust out this shit! Plus, momma told me never stop until I bust a nut. Fuck the world if they can't adjust! It's just a well. Hail Mary!
(Hook)

Penitentiaries are packed with promise makers. Never realizing the precious time these bitch niggas is wastin'. Institutionalized! I live my life a product made to crumble, but too hardened for a smile but too crazy to be humble. We ballin! Catch me Father please cause I'm fallin. In the liquor store, pass the Hennessy I hear it callin', can I get some more? Bail til I reach Hell, I ain't scared. Momma checkin' in my bedroom, I aint there! I got a head with no screws in it. What can I do? One life to live but I got nothin' to lose. Just me and you, on a way trip to prison. Sellin' drugs, we all wrapped up in this living. Life as thugs! To my homeboys in Quentin max doing' their bid, raise Hell to this real shit, and feel this. When you turn out the lights, I will be there in the dark, thuggin eternal through my heart. Now Hail Mary Nigga!

(Hook)

We've been travelling on this weary road. Long time life will be our heavy load. But we ride it, ride it like a bullet. Hail Mary. Hail Mary. We won't worry, everything will come real. We'll be free like the bird in the tree. We won't worry everything will come real, if we free like a bird in the tree. We're runnin' from the penitentiary. This is the time for the Liberty. Hail Mary. Hail Mary.

Come with me! Hail Mary. Nigga run quick see. What do we have here now? Do you wanna ride or die? West Side, Outlawz, Makaveli the Don, Solo, Killuminati, 7 Days.

Let's Talk About it

Hail Mary is one of Tupac's in-your-face pieces, hitting on religion and the written word of the Bible. The timing of this song's public release was eerie because it was released just a couple of months after his murder, and more so, the album cover depicted Tupac as a man crucified on the cross. Some say that the infamous hook "Hail Mary…. come quick see" is based on the words spoken by Jesus' disciples at the time they realized the body of Jesus no longer laid in his final resting place post-crucifixion but had indeed risen from the grave.

The King James version of the Bible states, *"Then go quickly and tell his disciples: He has risen from the dead and is going ahead of you unto Galilee. There you will see him. Now I have told you."* Christianity is based on the resurrection of Christ and the Holy Trinity. Jesus, in his lifetime, taught the Laws of Moses. Mary, the mother of Jesus, is highly regarded in the Catholic faith and has a prayer dedicated to her grace, power and mercy.

The Hail Mary prayer reads as follows: *"Hail Mary, full of Grace. The Lord is with thee. Blessed art thou amongst women and blessed is the fruit of thy womb, Jesus. Holy Mary, Mother of God, pray for us sinners, now and at the hour of our death. Amen."* Islam also recognizes the birth of Jesus in its religious texts; it refers to him as a prophet, not the son of God and doesn't agree that through him is the only way to salvation. Hebrew texts also give reference to the coming of the son of God.

It is well-known that Tupac was an avid and voracious reader. He read the Bible and other religious text several times throughout the course of his life. Considered in conjunction with the Makaveli 7 Day Theory album cover, it is apparent that this hook came from his intimate knowledge of the written word. This may imply that he wanted to express that he feels he has been a living victim of crucifixion by society and the mainstream media because he felt unsupported during his rape turned disorderly conduct trial.

Tupac endured negative assumptions and opinions about his purpose, intentions and meaning during his lifetime. He is indeed the *Rose that Grew from Concrete*. There were a few that took the time to get to know him and his body of work and accomplishments, but there were many with false assumptions or even no opinion at all. His catalog represents the past, present, and future. The past, because of his activism and civil rights lineage, the present because he still has a recognizable fan base, and also the future because he will most likely continue to have an impact on our youth and hip-hop culture.

You can't measure Tupac based on his lyrics alone, that would be unfair to those that love him and even more unfair to those that don't, because it will only add on to ignorance. You must begin pre-conception, to fully appreciate this man and understand what this world has lost due to his untimely death. He is the son of a prominent Black Panther Party member, Afeni Shakur and raised by civil rights activists who were a part of the heart of the civil rights movement for equality. Tupac was raised in the presence of this dialogue and sacrifice, so it makes sense that he brought this significant part of his childhood into his adult life.

Tupac stated in the opening lines of this song that, "God shall send his only begotten son to leave the wild from the ways of the man." This is a Christian belief, but Tupac stated on occasions that while he believed in God and prayed, he did not claim a religion. However, his relationship and belief in God is apparent through the pages of his published work. His conflict with God is also apparent.

In Tupac's song *Blasphemy* he states, "If Jesus was a kind man, then he should understand times in this crime land (my thug nation), do what you gotta do but know you gotta change, try and find a way to make it out the game. I leave this here and hope God can see my heart is pure. Is Heaven just another door?"

In another of Tupac's great songs, *Who Do You Believe In*, he is having a conversation with God, and he says, "So I'm asking, before I lay me down to sleep, before you judge me, look at all the shit you done to me, my misery. I rose up from the slums, made it out the flames, in my search for fame will I change? I am asking!"

Discussion

1. Do you believe that God loves men like Tupac?
2. Do you believe that God only serves those who have no sin?
3. Does a person with no sin exist?
4. Do you believe that God sent his only begotten son for men like Tupac?
5. Do you believe God has mercy for the man that lives in contradiction to His word?
6. Are there degrees to sin?
7. Should there be a tolerance for crime behavior if you were born into certain communities?

Tupac has millions of fans across the globe of many different faiths, but they relate to Tupac, this man who professes his own complicated relationship with God.

1. Do you believe that music, and a once in a lifetime musician like Tupac, have a way of breaking down barriers, boundaries and stereotypes?
2. Can we learn from music and take advantage of the benefits of what Tupac's music has to offer?

3. Consider Woodstock - do you feel it had an impact on breaking down race and class barriers?

4. Should your religion dictate your music choice?

Tupac states, "revenge is like the sweetest joy next to getting pussy."

1. What are your thoughts on revenge?

2. Can you think of an example in which revenge can be justified?

3. Can revenge be rewarding?

4. Does revenge come with consequences?

5. Should revenge come with consequences?

6. Once revenge starts, how does it stop?

7. What are some options for revenge?

Does it surprise you to hear Tupac say, "Bow down pray to God, hoping that he's listening?" He later states, "Hail Mary catch me if I go. Let's go deep inside the solitary mind of a madman who screams in the dark, enemies see me flee." Not many rappers address mental health in their lyrics. This verse of Tupac's could make someone say, I have those same thoughts and it is okay that I talk about it and get help. Ponder these lyrics above. Close your eyes and picture this person and create an image. What color and religion was the person you imagined? Why?

1. Does it matter to you what God looks like?

2. Does someone else's opinion of what God looks like matter to you?

3. Why did Tupac decide to reveal these deep inner thoughts to the world? Why does he want to take us to this spiritual place?

4. Should we try to understand the circumstances of a man screaming in the dark, living in a place where evil lurks, physically or mentally?

5. What are your thoughts on mental health services? How should they be paid?

6. Do people with untreated mental illnesses have an effect on your community?

7. What do you think your God would do regarding mental health?

Tupac goes on to say, "activate my hate." It may be a survival mechanism for Tupac rather than malicious intent to hurt or cause harm to someone, rather protect himself.

1. Can inner feelings of hate "protect" a person?

2. How can hate save you?

3. Ho can hate hurt you?

4. How does hate make you feel?

5. What do you hate? Why?

6. What or who hates you? Why?

Tupac continues with, "Penitentiaries are packed with promise makers. Never realizing the precious time these bitch niggas is wastin'. Institutionalized!" What does Tupac mean by "promise makers?" Does he mean the prisoners who are telling themselves, their families, the judge and society that they have indeed changed? Or could he mean the wardens, correction officers, and prison therapists who claim they care about their innocence and well-being? Could it be the penal system that tells the community that prison serves as a form of rehabilitation, a great source of revenue, and a great source of employment opportunities?

Institutionalized - what does this mean to you? Consider the movie *The Shawshank Redemption*, starring Morgan Freeman.   In the movie, Morgan's character, Red, is sentenced to life in prison as a teen. In one particular scene, Red speaks of an elderly fellow inmate and friend that had been originally sentenced to life but was being paroled after 40 years in prison. The paroled convict did not want to leave prison because he knew of no other way of living and surviving. Prison was the only life he knew. Red had referred to this man as being "institutionalized." In the movie, the paroled man committed suicide shortly after his release from jail. Can you imagine living a life where all you know is the penal system, a place where time stands still, and you are ruled over every minute of your very existence?

1. What are your thoughts on the penal system? Does it work?

2. What are the benefits of a life-term prison sentence?

3. Do politicians often speak of America's penal system? Why or why not?

4. Do you agree with Tupac's claim that there are prisoners in jail who don't realize the time they're wasting?

5. What does Tupac mean by "precious time?"

6. Do you believe that there are scholars who missed their opportunity and are spending their life in the penal system?

Drug dealers and offenders make up the majority in prison populations. Some dealers are self-educated mathematicians that have unfortunately applied this talent to their illegal trade. Many prisoners do not realize how smart they are and never realize that their genius can be applied to more stable and meaningful opportunities. There is an assumption that their intelligence is low because of their situation and that is usually a mistake. Most people may know of extremely talented people in varying fields that have no technical training. There are murderers in prison that due to their lack of self-control, lost out on their true calling in life. There are children in prison forced into adulthood because they never had an opportunity to freely perfect their God given craft with quality education and/or the guidance from a positive adult figure in their lifetime.

Tupac states, "I live my life a product made to crumble, but too hardened for a smile but too crazy to be humble." Let's assess this statement from the standpoint of product manufacturing. A product made to crumble by any means will fail the quality assurance standards that regulators require before a product goes to market. When a product is manufactured, it is presumed to be made of good quality, in a conducive environment, and made to last. A product "made to crumble" is a waste and if it was intended to crumble, the consumer has been duped. With enough customer complaints, charges may be brought upon its manufacturer. Tupac is speaking of human life though. The ghetto contains poor air and land quality, failing healthcare and school systems, and infrastructure and housing that are in dire need of repair. These conditions create "a product made to crumble".

Yet the expectation of society is that ghetto-born children should keep pace with peers born under more affluent conditions. The "ghetto" requires a "hardened" exterior, and humility may be seen as a sign of weakness. Many residents understand when he states that he's "too hardened for a smile but too crazy to be humble."

1. What social class might this person be from?

2. What are scenarios outside of low socioeconomic status that would make a person feel "like a product made to crumble"?

3. How can we foster healthier children?

4. Are people products of their environments?

This song continues with Tupac stating "Catch me Father please, cause I'm fallin'. In the liquor store, pass the Hennessy, I hear it callin', can I get some more?" Rev. Dr. Martin Luther King, Jr., once said, "every man must decide whether he will walk in the light of creative altruism or in the darkness of destructive selfishness." Many of us struggle with this on a day-to-day basis, and Tupac was no exception.   Has society set up our youth for failure with the seduction of sex, drugs, and alcohol on radio and television?   Tupac recognized this struggle of mankind and had numerous conversations with God. He readily admits his sins and his desire to remain connected to and not forgotten by God.

1. Do you confront your sins and verbally admit to them?

2. Do you recognize when you are heading in the wrong direction, or "falling" as Tupac referred to it?

3. In your conversations with your God, do you ask for forgiveness? Forgiveness for what?

4. Do you than change your behavior?

Tupac goes on in the song and states, "Momma checkin' in my bedroom, I ain't there! I got a head with no screws in it. What can I do? One life to live but I got nothin' to lose. Just me and you, on a one-way trip to prison. Sellin' drugs, we all wrapped up in this living. Life as thugs!" Society often blames parents for children who make bad decisions, and sometimes that is certainly the case, but even then there is often a deeper underlying cause that may go back generations. There are mothers and fathers that enforce good morals, discipline and goals into their children and these children still stray. Tupac is speaking of the mother checking in her child's bedroom, and the child is not there as expected to be. All of us have or know of these stories, children who grew up too fast or in crisis and went down a wrong path, and these cross all financial classes.

Youth today have a better chance of having a melting pot of friend "types" and to some degree, should have exposure to thieves, whores, drug users and lawbreakers. Without that exposure and the opportunity to make good decisions and some mistakes in their youth, how will they identify and know how to remove themselves from these types when they grow older? For example, a child that never saw a crack addict has no fear of crack.

Tupac's admission of "having a head with no screws in it" speaks of a person that is not in denial. St. Augustine once said, "this is the very perfection of a man, to find out his own imperfections." Tupac strived to be a strong man who was unafraid of the reflection in the mirror.

1. How do you feel about your reflection in the mirror? Do you feel society judges it the same way?

2. Have you ever defied your parent's rules? Where does bad behavior come from?

3. How exposed to bad behavior were you in your youth? Did it help or hurt your decision-making later in life?

4. Do you know of any children who are or were on a road to self-destruction, but were raised in a hands-on, overall loving family?

5. Do you ever give thought to the child that is forced to grow up too fast?

6. What are long-term consequences of growing up too fast? How can we help these children?

Tupac closes this song by saying, "When you turn out the lights, I will be there in the dark, thuggin' eternal through my heart. Now Hail Mary nigga." This verse stood out to most because of his murder prior to the release of this record. Many of his followers believe that he either knew his time on earth was coming to a near end, or that he was planning to fake his death. The dark can be a scary place and it seems he wanted his listeners to know he is with them.

1. Do you think Tupac knew that his living days were coming to an end?

2. Can death be foretold? Do you know of any examples?

3. Have you ever felt motivated because something told you to do it?

4. How do you want to be remembered?

5. How will you most likely be remembered?

The song comes to an end with a voice of a man saying "we've been travelling down this weary road. Long time life will be our heavy load. But we ride it, ride it like a bullet. Hail Mary. Hail Mary." Long time life is referred to as a heavy load. To live is to carry a weight on our shoulders, some a lot heavier than others.

1. What causes this difference in weight? Is it a personal choice?

2. Do we choose the lives we lead?

3. Does a child born into poverty or with an absent parent have the same opportunities as the child born in a middle class or upper society family with both parents?

Imagine if your sole providing parent was an active revolutionary like Afeni or Assata Shakur, or Angela Davis among others. These women and mothers each spent their lives fighting for equality and justice, while being largely apart from their own children. The sacrifice is unappreciated and unknown by most of this generation.

1. Are there strong women that you look up to?

2. Should women have the same rights as men?

3. Would you spend a considerable amount of time away from your family to protest or take a stand for a cause that you strongly believe in?

4. What if the children of protestors or activists go astray? Would you blame the parents, or would you consider the sacrifices made by the parents?

5. Do you consider the history of a child who has gone astray?

THE BLACK PANTHER
25 cents
Black Community News Service
THE BLACK PANTHER PARTY
REVOLUTIONARY PEOPLE'S
CONSTITUTIONAL CONVENTION
HOWARD UNIVERSITY
WASHINGTON, D.C.
NOVEMBER 27, 28 & 29, 1970
HUEY P. NEWTON, MINISTER OF DEFENSE
WILL READ THE PEOPLE'S NEW CONSTITUTION

Military Minded

Tupac Shakur, Better Dayz (Disc II)

Stand in formation my motherfuckin' real troopers. Let's do it like soldiers! All in together now. Ready? Hell yeah! No retreat no surrender. Death before dishonor motherfucker! Do it to 'em. Do it to 'em. West side East side we ride. Where you at? Where you at? Where my real thugs? Where you at? Where you at? Where my real thugs? Where you at? Where you at? Where my real thugs? Where you at? Where you at? The cases of a drug dealer. Real thugs, where you at? A motherfuckin' army. Do it to 'em. Do it to 'em. They love the way we do it to 'em.

Suppress the revolution of a premeditated scheme, introduce this drug called crack to us ghetto teens. Got a law for real niggaz now. Playa what it be like? When will they see they got us bleeding with three strikes? Can't seem to focus, hopeless, with violent thoughts I wrote this. Got these devils petrified hiding from my hocus pocus. And so I learned to earn my currency over time, affiliated clearly clicked a military mind.

May God forgive me, though we dwell inside a paradox. Thugged out and drug dealin' from the womb to the block. My live mind got me surviving 5 shots. My 45 got me fortified with live shots. When shit's thick, we plot hits, when our block spits, all hail, out on bail, wrath of 2pacalypse. Forever ghetto, necessary get your food stamps. Outlaw thug niggaz, never left the boot camp."

(Outro) Yeah! And this is how we do it! Where my real thugs? Where they at? Where they at? Let me see my real thugs! Where you at? Where my soldiers? Where you at? Where you at? Get your thugs! Where you at with your strap? Where my soldiers? Where my true thug niggas? No longer drug dealers, cause we now thug niggas!! Where my soldiers at? Put your pistols in the air! Where my soldiers at? Put your pistols in the air! Where my soldiers at? Fuck what you heard! From the ghetto to the burbs, know we meant every word. When Bob Dole and Delores Tucker wanna know where my soldiers at, GO VOTE!

Let's Talk About it

This song is a passionately written and presented piece of work that represents Tupac's frustration and his undeniable quest for survival and confronting oppression head-on. In line with Tupac's upbringing, he knows from a very early age that history has taught us that revolutionaries hold a deep and meaningful part of every oppressed people's existence. It includes "standing in- formation" literally and metaphorically with your peers. In order for a revolution to be deemed necessary, the root of its foundation is typically suffering to an extreme degree that will make one give their life for a cause, ending the control of the oppressor.

He starts out this song with, "suppress the revolution, a premeditated scheme, introduce a drug called crack to us ghetto teens." It's a powerful opening line to a song riddled with calls for the people to open their eyes.

Discussion

1. To whose or what revolution is he referring to?
2. Tupac states "suppression of the revolution, a premeditated scheme." Who do you think Tupac believes is behind this scheme?
3. Does it matter what the fight for change is about in order for you to have compassion?
4. Does oppression have to meet an acceptable standard for the world to embrace its elimination?
5. What if this resistance to oppression, happens to oppress another group?

In the late 60's and early 70's, the black and brown generations' "revolution" was at its peak. There was a sharp rise in the black community's disdain for unfair and unjust treatment. The fight for personal freedoms and safety, self-respect, along with a hate for the injustice and racial crimes committed against people of color that were hardly reprimanded in America. During these years, several prominent civil rights organizations joined the fight for change, including the likes of the National Association for the Advancement of Colored People (NAACP), The Urban League, SCLC (The Southern Christian Leadership Council), founded by Rev. Dr. Martin Luther King, Jr., and the Student Non-Violent Coordinating Committee

(SNCC), once chaired by a young John Lewis, who went on to later serve in the United States Congress until his death in 2020. These new, young, boisterous, and progressive organizations shared a non-violent philosophy for their demand for respect, civil rights, and personal freedoms that should be awarded to all men. They did not believe in, nor adhere to any notion of violence against violence. An eye for an eye, defend yourself and family at all costs, even with your very own life, was not their stance. These groups mirrored the approach of Rev. Dr. Martin Luther King, Jr. vs. Malcolm X or the Black Panther Party (BPP).

Revolutionary Ernesto "Che" Guevara once asked, "Why does the guerilla fighter fight? We must come to the inevitable conclusion that the guerilla fighter is a social reformer, that he takes up arms responding to the angry protest of the people against their oppressors, and that he fights in order to change the social system that keeps all his unarmed brothers in ignominy and misery."

There are several recommended reads about these powerful freedom fighters. Beginning with Civil Rights era books, the autobiography of The Black Panther Party titled Seize the Time is the perfect start on this quest for understanding the history, purpose, and reason for the current fears of the black family in America. Then move on to the biographies of Assata Shakur, Afeni Shakur, Fred Hampton, Mumia Abu Jamal, Elaine Brown, Soul on Ice by then-Panther member Eldridge Cleaver, Long Time Gone by Panther William Lee Brent, The Briar Patch by Murray Kempton, The Wretched of the Earth by Frantz Fanon, and Blood in my Eye by George L. Jackson.

In time, the government, led by President Ronald Reagan and CIA Director J. Edgar Hoover dismantled militant style activist groups, via infiltration, murder, lies, set-ups, uncountable raids, and the introduction of drugs such as crack. Director J. Edgar Hoover said at one time, "The Breakfast for Children Program represents the best and the most influential activity going for the BPP and, as such, is potentially the greatest threat to efforts by authorities to neutralize the BPP and destroy what it stands for."

Today's youth largely do not seem to be aware of or appreciate the rise and struggle of these freedom fighters who are today largely gone. Why is this? Many American adults can relate to the memory of their parents refusal to speak of their past.   "It's just too painful," many of our parents have said and this is the way many were taught to handle pain, do not speak on it. It's an understandable defense mechanism, but the result is that future generations have not learned to appreciate the hardship and sacrifice of our ancestors or the power of activism to create real change. Perhaps the same has happened here; in an effort to protect our youth, we have enabled oppression and injustice.

1. Is it best for our elders to teach us about our dark past or to shield us?

It is widely acknowledged even in the media and the government that the Vietnam War went on as long as it did because American media did not report on it, due to its gruesomeness. Once the horrific pictures and the stories became public, average Americans began a call to end the war. Until then, the mass concern over this war was out of sight, out of mind. It was not until the information was shared amongst the general public that the activists became empowered and were able to force an end to the war. I wonder, could the approach of this old school generation, whose intent was to save us post-70's babies from the pain they endured, actually have shielded us to such an extent that it created pure ignorance and a lack of appreciation for the blood-soaked sacrifice of our ancestors, as well as the power of activism?

Regardless, conversations with the elderly can teach us a lot. There are scores of books to teach us, so we can still educate ourselves on what happened in our past. Social media has helped a lot of the younger generations become more aware and vocally active. The awareness for wanting stronger communities for all and the political power required for those initiatives to succeed has brought a lot of young people to the forefront. Youth of today are really engaged in the areas of gun rights and control, personal and quality healthcare, climate change, LGBT rights and a growing number are becoming engaged in the fairness of our judicial system.

Tupac believed the introduction of crack was premeditated (and there is evidence he was correct); when he stated, "introduce a drug called crack to us ghetto teens." Crack is a cooked form of cocaine. Cocaine is the oldest known psychoactive drug, and the coca leaf that it is made from, is not grown or manufactured in the ghetto. Cocaine was first separated from the coca leaf around 1860 by scientist named Albert Nieman for medicinal purposes such as anesthesia.

Soon after, the scientific community discovered cocaine's addictive and devastating power to cause great harm to people. In 1914, the Harrison Act banned the social use of cocaine and other substances in non-prescription products after it plagued the lives of many people, (at that time, primarily Europeans). Crack cocaine suddenly reappeared in the ghettos in the late 1970's, possibly due to the crackdown of pure cocaine in the 1960's that terrorized suburban and socialite party towns. Crack, made from cocaine was largely produced in order to have a cheaper, easier transportable drug, that can be distributed quickly but this was also very addictive. It hit communities of color with massive devastation.

The reemergence of this powerful drug coinciding with the rise of the civil rights movement devastated even more inner-city families. The 1973 Rockefeller Law, named after the then-governor of New York, limited a judge's ability to assign a low crime drug offender to rehabilitation rather than prison. The government pushed for imprisonment of minor drug offenses instead of rehabilitation. Under the law "the penalty for selling 2 ounces (57g) or more of heroin, morphine, 'raw or prepared opium', cocaine, or cannabis or possessing 4 ounces (113g) or more of the same substances," was a minimum of fifteen years to life in prison, and a maximum of 25 years to life in prison. This law was especially harmful to black and brown communities and has gone through a series of government reforms as it became apparent that this law was unjust. Tupac continues in the song "introduce this drug called crack to us ghetto teens" and "when will they see they got us bleeding with three strikes?

1. How do you suppose crack cocaine made its way into the inner cities?
2. How do you think drugs get transported throughout America? Where are most of these grown?
3. What and where is the war Tupac is referring to the preparation of in the song "Military Minded"?
4. How does war typically begin? How does war typically end?

Tupac refers to guns often in this piece. For example, he states, "My 45 got me fortified with live shots." We have seen the popular pictures of the BPP and the Proud Boy types of organizations, both exercising their right to bear arms in public.

1. Why would a law-abiding person want to own a gun?
2. Do you own a gun?
3. Do you support gun control laws?
4. Should military-grade weapons be banned from civilian use? What is your opinion on them?
5. Do you know the current gun laws in your district? Are you satisfied with them?
6. What is your position on military grade weapons such as AR-15's? Vest piercing bullets?
7. If you or a loved one were a victim of a gun, would you support the Second Amendment?
8. Do you support civilian law enforcement?
9. Do citizens with the right to bear arms have a right to act as civilian law enforcement?
10. Are there scenarios in which you would or would not support this form of civilian activism?
11. How far do you believe a person has a right to go to protect their or their neighbor's property?

Tupac states, "When will they see they got us bleeding with three strikes, can't seem to focus. Hopeless. With violent thoughts I wrote this." The Three Strikes law came into existence on November 4, 1994 and meant that people with three felonies are to be sentenced with a 25 year to life in prison.

1. What are pros of the Three Strikes law? Cons?
2. What about stop and frisk laws?
3. If you are not very familiar with either of these laws, why might that be? Do some research on them, if necessary, and discuss what you think of them.

4. Have you known anyone to be sentenced under these guidelines? What was the situation?

5. Do you think this law has created a change in repeat offenders?

Tupac later states, "forever ghetto, necessary get your food stamps." Poverty is defined as the state of having little or no money and few or no material possessions.

1. What is your definition of poverty?

2. If you were not born into poverty, how do you imagine your life and personality would be different if you had been?

3. Do you agree that positive outlets like hobbies, role models, and community-based organizations are helpful to grow people out of the ghetto?

4. How can we improve upon our "outlets" for our youth? How do we assist those that are born into these conditions of poverty, and despair?

5. How can the United States of America, recognized as one of the wealthiest and strongest nations in the world, eliminate poverty? Is that a goal and should it be?

6. How can we kill the root of poverty? i.e., the generational cycle improper housing, inadequate education and healthcare, broken families, crime and drug abuse.

7. As a nation, can we identify those who will benefit from aid from those who have simply suffered too much for a full recovery into a peaceful mainstream society?

Reportedly, there are more guns than humans; and simply put, rhetoric aside, this means that there is a war going on in the streets of America and we are either soldiers or civilians. A soldier is defined as an enlisted man or woman who serves in an army. A civilian is a noncombatant member of society. Guns are prevalent in both groups.

Before and during the Civil War era, the right to bear arms was practiced by everyone, including black people in order to defend against the likes of ex-slave masters, and other violent racist groups. However, now it seems that this this right has moved to senseless violence, turf wars, political discourse, gang initiations, and genocide. Mass murder in this generation has often committed by school aged children, and more recently there has been a reported rise in white adult males. In regard to the black and brown communities, somewhere this generation has lost sight of what the common goal of equality and justice had been since slavery began in 1619, it was forged in community survival - certainly not murdering each other. These guns, used to colonize and own Africa and many other nations through the trade of British made guns for African slaves, are now celebrated in urban culture and communities.

Tupac stated, "my live mind got me surviving five shots." Tupac indeed had been shot five times, so gun violence was a reality for him despite his wealth. On the evening of November 30, 1994, Tupac was shot and robbed as he entered Quad Recording Studios in Times Square NYC. In remembering the New York Times photo of Tupac being rolled into the ambulance from the crime scene on a stretcher, he raised his middle finger to the cameramen, responding to the indecency of the photographer documenting his condition while in crisis.

He was rushed to Bellevue Hospital where he was operated on, and he later discharged himself against doctor's orders the very next day. In this verse, Tupac suggests that his mental strength and capacity contributed to his survival, yet earlier in this song he refers to feeling hopeless. This contrast suggests that along with the physical and mental strength required of a person being raised and living in impoverished neighborhoods or under tough circumstances, there are a wide range of other emotions and feelings as well.

1. Should a person growing up in the ghetto and a person growing up in the suburbs be expected to reason and react the same way? Why or why not?
2. Can you understand how these individuals could view the world differently?
3. How often do you stop and imagine the world from someone else's point of view?
4. Are you open to consider other ways of thinking?
5. How can we bridge the divide and better understand not just what we have in common but where we are also different? Is it too late for that?

Tupac created acronyms for "Thug Life" and "Nigga" - The Hate U Give to Little Infants Fucks Everyone and Never Ignorant, Getting Goals Accomplished.

1. Does this change your thoughts or opinion of what Tupac meant by expressing "thug life" often? What about the word "nigga"?
2. Do you see a difference in Tupac's reference of drug dealers and thug niggas, with this insight?
3. Have you ever considered that poverty and war are similar?

Tupac ends this very deep and emotional song with two everlasting and timeless words, GO VOTE! We live in an America that saw a 1-year congressmen Barack Obama serve two full terms followed by President Donald Trump, a businessman and reality TV star - then followed by the election of President Obama's vice president to President, with the first female and person of color as Vice President. These are two, arguably three, very different ideologies.

1. Do you consider what side of history you will be standing on when you take political or moral positions?
2. What do you think of the integrity of America's democratic voting process?
3. Would you personally help youth to vote, and how?
4. Is there an honor associated with accepting losing in a competition?
5. What is your definition of a Free and Democratic state?
6. Should Presidential election day be a Federal Holiday?

Time Period Reference Photos

THE INTRODUCTION, PROFESSOR TURNER TERRACE

Black Panthers NEED Bail Money

THE 18 ADULT BLACK PANTHERS ARRESTED IN SACRAMENTO MAY 2 WERE FALSELY CHARGED WITH CONSPIRACY TO DISRUPT THE ASSEMBLY. THE BAIL FOR EACH PANTHER WAS $2,200.00, TOTALLING $40,000.00. THE PANTHERS NEED THREE THOUSAND DOLLARS MORE OF THE FOUR THOUSAND DOLLAR 10% BAIL FEE. BROTHERS AND SISTERS HELP US. BONDSMAN GOT US IN A BIND. SEND ALL BAIL MONEY DONATIONS TO:

RILY ON THE FACT THAT THEY ARE ORGAN-IZED AND UNITED WITH EACH OTHER. THEY ARE RECOGNIZED BY ALL THE POWERS OF THE WORLD. WE WITH ALL OUR NUMBERS

Black Panther Party
• For Self Defense
• P.O. Box 8641 EMERYVILLE Br.
Oakland CALIF., 94608

THESE COURAGEOUS BLACK BROTHERS, THE HEROES OF MAY 2 BLACK PANTHER DAY, UNDERSTOOD THE SIGNIFICANCE OF GOING TO THE CAPITOL, ARMED TO THE GILL, TO DELIVER A MESSAGE TO THE BLACK WORLD ON WHITE RACISM.

BLACK GI'S BATTLE
ON THE HOME FRONT

The following statement was issued by the Fort Hood United Front, in Killeen, Texas. The fact that the racist practices of the U.S. government are firmly planted in the military forces of this country, should come as no surprise. Black people are suffering, as a whole, daily oppression due to overt racism, that is part of the "American way". If we can understand being the "last hired and the first fired", we can certainly grasp the fact that Black men are the first in the U.S. military to be sent to fight and die. Black people really have no business in the U.S. military. For what reason should any of our people commit ourselves to defend the interests of the United States. It is only logical

to say that we would be defending the interests of those who oppress us. Black GI's are beginning to truly realize this, as the statement indicates, and are beginning to struggle against the racist and fascist policies of the U.S. military:

What may well develop into a post-wide Black organization to combat racism on Ft. Hood was sparked November 15 by the visit of Representative Louis Stokes , a member of the Congressional Black Caucus. Stokes came to Ft. Hood to begin hearings on racism in the military. The hearings, conducted by the Black Caucus, will continue, on November 16th to 18th, in Washington, D.C.

The organization, called the Peoples' Justice Committee (PJC), was formed when it became obvious in the course of the hearing that simply talking with Rep. Stokes would not solve the problems of racism in the military. The Brothers decided that what was needed was a strong, independent organization of Black enlisted men that could defend and support itself.

In a press release issued by the Black Caucus before the hearing, "military justice" was cited as one of the things the Caucus would be seriously investigating. "For instance, Black GI's represent 30.6% of the population of the Army's world wide confinement facilities and in the Air Force they represent the incredible figure of 53.4% of the inmates of this service's confinement facilities. Similarly the Navy and Marine Corps have in their stockades a disproportionate number of Black GI's, these figures being 16.2% and 21.0% respectively. Additional reason for concern in this area is the too frequent occasion of lily-white justice. Blacks constitute less than 1% of the military lawyers and little is being done to correct this situation. " To say the least, those words were proven true at today's hearing (November 15th).

The stage was set by the Brass's blatant refusal to provide decent facilities for the hearing. In a letter to General George Seneff (commander of Ft. Hood), Rep. Ronald Dellums of the Black Caucus asked,"That Rep. Stokes be provided with a theater or meeting room capable of seating at least 200 persons." Yet when GI's began arriving at the appointed place for the hearing in the morning, they were handed numbers and told they would be talking with Rep. Stokes "one at a time". But the 100-150 people who gathered decided they would rather talk in a group, and Stokes agreed. So the hearing was moved to a condemned barracks that was no longer in daily use.

Most of those in attendance had been informed of the hearing by members of the Ft. Hood United Front, who had worked with Stokes to co-ordinate the activities. The Army, although it had received advance word of the hearing and its nature, put out little if any publicity. Some companies were told at morning formation that Stokes would be on fort, and anyone who wanted to could go talk with him. But no mention was made of the fact that he had come to investigate racism.

Before the hearing began, the press was asked to leave by the brothers who had come to testify. Most had seen how the press had handled the question of racism in the past, and all were aware of the repercussions that would come as a result of them appearing in local media. The reporter for the Fatigue Press, Ft. Hood's GI newspaper, was allowed to stay.

CONTINUED ON NEXT PAGE

(Lyrics to)

Fame

Tupac Shakur, Better Days (Disc II)

And my nigga say…..We want the FAME! C'mon C'mon

One thing we all adore. Something worth dying for. Nothin' but pain, stuck in the game, searching for fortune and FAME.

One thing we all adore. Something worth dying for. Nothin' but pain, stuck in the game, searching for fortune and FAME.

Though we exist and breathe, some believe currency comes to G's. Stress is half the battle, with success comes greed. They got me hot when they shot me. Plotted my revenge to increase my ends, enemies getting dropped. Win or lose, red or blue, we must all stay true. Play the game nigga!! Never let the game play you. And for the fame, nigga's change fast. That's a shame. What's to gain, lost souls who control our brains? Who can I blame? The world seems strange at times, somewhat insane. I'm hoping we can change with time. I'm living blinded, searching for a refinement curse. I know death follows me, but I murder him first. And worse yet, with each breath, steps I take. Breathless! Is there a cure for a hustler with a death wish? Cigar ashes, coastin', crystal glass, we mashin' on them jealous bastards, with my ski mask. I'm the first one to warn and blast it, wrapped in plastic. Bullshittin' got his ass hit. Ain't nothin' left now. Treated like a stepchild and was not for me nothing but busters and bitches. Be rockin' beats, faking fame. (check)

(Chorus)
One thing we all adore. Something worth dying for. Nothin' but pain, stuck in the game, searching for fortune and FAME.

Let's Talk About it

I think we can all agree that artists and celebrities pay a heavy price for "fortune and fame." Tupac said in *Me Against the World*, "if I'm insane, it's the fame that made a brother change, it wasn't nothin' like the game. It's just me against the world." Fame is coveted, but there are many examples where it is devastating. Fortune and fame can turn a poor man rich and a rich man poor. It can heal the heart of a person and can break the heart of the same. Fortune and fame can move mountains and can make it seem that a mountain has moved on top of you. What does fame mean to you?

How well a person adapts to fame likely is often related to how that fame was obtained. A child born into fame by way of celebrity parents may have a better chance at adapting to the lifestyle. It may be a good life or a bad life, but nonetheless, it is the only life they know. A person thrust into fortune and fame may have a greater risk of failure in this new life.

Tupac faced controversy in part because he did not separate the mindset of the "movement" and the poverty he was raised in from all the fortunes gained from the somewhat overnight fame brought to him. Tupac carried the badge and scars of being brought up deep in the heart of the civil rights movement. Tupac survived being raised in the ghetto, he loved and hated the ghetto, and he felt bound to it. He had been influenced by the same prominent and powerful Black Panthers and activists that made real change in America. He grew up admiring them but later watched a lot of them fall victim to government infiltration or self-destruction.

Activists such as George Jackson, author of the most notable *Blood in My Eye*, was assassinated in prison by guards while serving an 18+ year prison sentence. Bunchy Carter, a young prominent Black Panther, was murdered in cold blood by the LAPD. Assata Shakur, also a prominent Black Panther, now lives in exile in Cuba after being wrongfully convicted of the murder of a New Jersey State Trooper in what was said to be a biased and unfair trial. Huey P. Newton, co-founder of the Black Panther Party, empowered tens of thousands of people young and old of all races and cultures, to care about themselves, their community, and their rights, their education, health, the poor, liberty and justice, he later fell victim to drugs. The list of influences Tupac grew up with ranges from his own mother, Afeni Shakur, to H. Rap Brown, Elaine Brown, Angela Davis, Sekou Odinga, and Mumia Abu Jamal.

These family members and comrades became political prisoners, murder victims, exiles, drug addicts and several success stories.

By the time Tupac was a rapper he knew about fame, and he knew about falls from grace because of the movement and era he was raised in. Then comes the "price" for fortune and fame. What is the price for fortune and fame? To some the price of fame could be the non-stop media and paparazzi attention, the lack of privacy in your life, or not having a place to call home because of travel and demands of your schedule.

Some of white America was angered by the strength of The Black Panther Party and other such groups, as they began achieving goals on their way to equality, justice, and liberty for all. Because of his mother Afeni's revolutionary involvement with the Panther 21 trial, where she successfully defended herself against trumped-up charges that would have landed her over 300 years in prison, her fame made the media paint her as a danger to society. She was forced to leave New York, where she migrated through Montclair, New Jersey, into Maryland, and ultimately all the way to California.

Through this, funds were very low and Tupac with his beautiful dark skin, grew up very poor during a period when racism was rampant. In the song White Man'z World he wrote, "Momma why they keep on calling me nigga? Get my hate up with my weight and pay 'em back when I'm bigger!" In those few words, Tupac summed up the cause of so much anger still lingering in Black America, and it still may be what is the most misunderstood by mainstream America.

Afeni faced struggles after the infamous Panther 21 trial, and Tupac turned to the streets, at that time unaware of or out of touch with his talent. Tupac's childhood was embedded in The Black Panther Party movement, he was unsure of his natural father but had admiration for the men in his life, specifically Mumia Abu Jamal and Lumumba Shakur. Tupac, was a heavy load to carry. He spoke with such authenticity, bearing his own soul in the process, leaving raw parts of him behind, just for his internal machine to rebuild him, so that he can give and give again. Tupac is a well with no bottom, a river with no shores, the sun with no boundaries of its light. Tupac is timeless and endless, forever accessible to all those that listen.

Tupac opens this song with the chorus "One thing we all adore. Something worth dying for. Nothin' but pain, stuck in the game, searching for fortune and fame".

Discussion

1. Have you ever experienced the feeling of being stuck? Think about debt, an unhappy job, marriage, or friendship. How can you change that feeling within yourself

2. Is fortune and fame worth dying for?

3. What is Tupac referring to in this verse when he uses the word "game"? One tends to think of winners and losers or for the need for strategic thought. Why did he use that word instead of another?

4. Is life a game?

5. What pain could Tupac be referring to?

6. Why do some people adapt well to fame and others seem to ruin themselves by behaving recklessly?

7. Have you ever wanted to be famous?

8. What is usually sacrificed for fame?

Tupac continues in this song with "Though we exist and breathe, some believe currency comes to G's. Stress is half the battle, with success comes greed."

1. Tupac appears to be saying that stress is easier to deal with than the greed that may come along with success. What is your interpretation?

2. Can success turn to greed? How?

3. Greed is one of the deadly sins. Why?

4. How can power be abused?

5. Should there always be a check against Power? Is one man above the law?

6. Can being successful give you an overstated sense of power?

Tupac goes on to write, "Plotted my revenge to increase my ends, enemies getting dropped. Win or lose, red or blue, we must all stay true. Play the game nigga, never let the game play you."

1. How can revenge increase ends (money)? Is revenge ever a good thing?

2. In the second sentence, this can be interpreted as advice. But to whom? The community, corporate America, politicians, businessmen, thugs and/or scholars, someone else?

3. When and where is this way of thought appropriate? Politics? Marriage? Family relationships? Anywhere?

Tupac continues in this song with "I know death follows me, but I murder him first?" Outside of outright murder, this verse can also mean street survival, competitive sports, or a person surrounded by a failing school system, yet they make a personal goal to exceed and become highly educated. It could mean a person raised in a drug dealing and using family and they break the chain by resisting drugs.

1. What does that statement mean to you?

2. Do you believe this statement is limited only to death?

3. What if this same statement had been written by a white poet or classic novelist? Would you apply the same interpretation?

Tupac than asks "Is there a cure for a hustler with a death wish?"

1. Is there someone you know that you think of when you hear the expression "death wish?" How do they live? Consider street life, drug use, promiscuity, overworking, or overindulgence.

2. Is there a cure, so to speak, for a death wish?

3. How can the community help? Or is it the government's problem?

4. Who are the victims of this hustler's way of thinking and living?

Tupac continues with this verse; "We mashin' on them jealous bastards, with my ski mask." A ski mask can be used for the correct purpose of course and also for a person to hide their identity. Consider the ski mask in its literal and nonliteral sense and interpret it as it relates to crime, friendships, co-workers, intimate relationships, shady business deals and corporate greed.

1. Do you really know the people you surround yourself with?

Tupac closed out this song with "Bullshitting got his ass hit." Bullshitting could be interpreted as lying, conniving, cheating, jive talking, simply procrastinating or not remaining aware of your surroundings.

1. What does this comment mean to you?
2. Can you apply this statement to your life or the life of a person that you know?

What Does This Mean to You II?

"I'll tell you what freedom is to me - no fear." - Nina Simone

"We might fight amongst each other, but I promise you this. We'll burn this bitch down if you get us pissed!" - Tupac Shakur

"Lord, I'm going to hold steady on to You and You've got to see me through." - Harriet Tubman

"Who do you believe in? I put my faith in God, blessed and still breathing. And even though it's hard, that's who I believe in. Before I am leaving, I'm asking the grieving, who do you believe in?" - Tupac Shakur

"I would fight for my liberty so long my strength lasted, and if the time came for me to go, the Lord would let them take me." - Harriet Tubman

"Men go abroad to wonder at the heights of mountains, at the huge waves of the sea, at the long courses of the rivers, at the vast compass of the ocean, at the circular motions of the stars, and they pass by themselves without wondering." - St. Augustine

"If Jesus was a kind man, then he should understand times in this crime land." - Tupac Shakur

"Pray as though everything depended on God. Work as though everything is dependent upon you." - St. Augustine

"Keep your head up and try to keep your faith and pray for better days." - Tupac Shakur

"America and Islam are not exclusive and need not be in competition. Instead, they overlap, and share common principles of justice and progress, tolerance and the dignity of all human beings." - Barack Obama

"Regard your soldiers as your children, and they will follow you into the deepest valleys. Look on them as your own beloved sons, and they will stand by you even unto death." - Sun Tzu

"Sister, sorry for the pain that I caused your heart. I know I'll change if you help me, but don't fall apart." - Tupac Shakur

"I want to be the white man's brother, not his brother-in-law." - Rev. Dr. Martin Luther King, Jr.

"Just lay your head on my shoulder, don't worry about a thing, baby girl. I am a soldier!"
- Tupac Shakur

"If two friends ask you to judge a dispute, don't accept, because you will lose one friend. On the other hand, if two strangers come with a request, accept because you will gain one friend." - St. Augustine

"You don't choose your family. They are God's gift to you, as you are to them." - Desmond Tutu

"The lack of emotional security of our American young people is due, I believe, to their isolation from the larger family unit. No two people - no mere father and mother - as I have often said, are enough to provide emotional security for a child. He needs to feel himself one in a world of kinfolk, persons of variety in age and temperament, and yet allied to himself by an indissoluble bond which he cannot break if he could, for nature has welded him into it before he was born." - Pearl S. Buck

"The worst solitude is to be destitute of sincere friendship." - Francis Buck

"You can't shake hands with a clenched fist." - Indira Gandhi

"I destroy my enemies when I make them my friends." - Abraham Lincoln

"Men are so simple and so much inclined to obey immediate needs that a deceiver will never lack victims for his deceptions." – Machiavelli

"And I will do everything that I can as long as I am President of the United States to remind the American people that we are one nation under God, and we may call that God different names, but we remain one nation." - Barack Obama

JOAN BIRD AND AFENI SHAKUR

Our Minister of Information, Eldridge Cleaver has said that women are not our weaker half, or our stronger half, they are our other half. We in the Black Panther Party do not relate to male chauvinism. When the fascist pig gestapo forces (FBI, CIA and state and local police) attack our people, in the colonies of North Amerikkka, they do not make a destinction between men and women. And many of our comrades, who are facing life imprisonment, or the death penalty, are women. Fourteen members of the New Haven Branch of the Black Panther Party (including our Chairman, Bobby Seale) were indicted for conspiracy to commit murder. Of the 14 Connecticut Panthers who have been

Afeni Shakur is not accused of having committed any crimes in the indictment. The only crime Afeni appears to be guilty of aside from being a hard working servant of the people - is that she is a beautiful writer (her "letters from jail" have appeared in the Black Panther Party black Community News Serivce on numerous occassions), an articulate speaker and a fromidable (to the pigs) organizer.

By indicting the N.Y. 21, the fascist pig power structure was trying to stop the implementation of the Free Breakfast for Children Program, in the N Y C. area. The national repression against the Party, can be directly linked to the spread of the Breakfast for Children Program. Just when the Breakfast Program was about to become a reality in New York, the N.Y 21 was framed. The FBI was going around the city bragging that "the Panthers in New York are finished." But the fascistic attempts to destroy the Party in New York, inpeded progress only momentarily; on May 19, 1969 the Harlem branch started its first Community Breakfast Program in honor of Malcolm X' s Birthday.

On October 8, 1969, Panther attorney, Gerald Lefcourt, informed us that the pigs were trying to get a new grand jury indictment against the N.Y. 21, and that it appeared so underhanded that two DA's had threatened to resign. The new indictment would

JOAN BIRD

N.Y. 21 GO ON TRIAL

It has been more than seven months since 21 members of the New York State Chapter of the Black Panther Party were indicted by a grand jury on trumped - up charges of conspiracy to blow-up department stores, railroad facilities and the Bronx Botanical Gardens. Thirteen Panthers are still being held in "preventive Detention," in lieu of a ransom of $100,000. each. They have had nineteen bail hearings, and each time, the fascist courts of New York city have refused to lower the ransom.

The bail system of fascist America was supposed to have been designed to insure the defendant's return to court and bail is usually granted, provided the arrested person is not considered to be a danger to the community. All of the N.Y. 21, up to the time of their arrest, were outstanding community workers and servants of the people. The astronimical ransom placed on the 21, and Panthers all across the country, (Landon Williams and Rory Hithe are being held for $200,000. each in Denver, Colorado) is nothing but a slick facade for "pretrial Detention." Convicted murders, while pending an appeal, can get out of jail on reasonable bails. But Freedom Fighters, who have not committed any crimes, are held for "king ransoms," which are tantamount to no bail at all.

Framing innocent dissenters and Black liberation fighters and railroading them to prison on jive conspiracy charges is nothing new in imperialist Amerikka. Our Minister of Defense, Huey P. Newton, was railroaded to jail by the racist pig courts in Alameda County, California. During the McCarthy era, conspiracy busts were used to imprison the leadership of the Communist Party, U.S.A. But New York, in particualr, has a long history of conspiracy busts. There's the Harlem Six in 1965. The plot to blow-up the Statue of Liberty in 1966. Seventeen members of Ram were indicted for conspiracy to assassinate moderate (uncle tom) civil rights leaders in 1967. And in 1968, five young brothers from Harlem were charged with conspiracy to break into armories and steal weapons and kill a pig a week. In 1969, the ball got to rolling with the N.Y. 21.

These thirteen political prisoners are being held in seven different jails in the New York city area. All of them have been subjected to "cruel and unusual punishment." The infamous "Tombs," however, is the worst of all the city jails. The Panthers who are jailed in the tombs are kept on 24-hour lock-up, the lighys in their cells remain on 24-hours a day, and they are only allowed to leave their cells to see visitors.

Lee Berry (who was kidnapped from a hospital bed on April 4, 1969), has had several epileptic seizures since he's been incarcerated in the Tombs. On July 23, 1969, Lee Berry suffered an epileptic seizure and while he was under the influence of medication, a racist pig (correction officer) ordered him to "get the f--k up." Still dazed, brother Lee Berry attempted to rise to his feet, and the gestapo pig guard drew a blackjack and commenced to beat him about the head.

Other Panther have been placed in the "bing" (solitary confinement) when caught reading the Party Paper. The N.Y.C. Department of Corrections had declared that the Black Panther Black Community News Service is contraband. All of the N.Y. 21, at one time or another, have been placed in the "bing", which includes 24-hour lock-up, no showers, no mail, no visits and no commissary privileges.

Acting on orders emanating from pig Nixon, via racist attorney general Mitchell, pig J.J. Hoffamn has set the precedent for the type of justice that all Black people will be the victims of in the criminal courts of dying Babylon. And we anticipate the

Bobby Seale charged with conspiracy to commit murder) the fascist courts of New Haven have already layed down the "ground rules". Everyone entering the courtroom will be searched. No cameras, tape recorders and no sketching will be allowed. All demonstrations will have to be held 500 feet away from the courthouse. On November 22, the New Haven Chapter of the Party has

held, without bail, since May 22, 1969, five are women. Three of the jailed sisters are pregnant with their first child.

Among the N.Y. 21, two of the members of the N.Y. 21 are women. They are Joan Bird and Afeni Shakur. On January 17, 1979 Joan Bird was found in a disabled car, near the scene of an alleged sniper attack on two pigs. Sister Joan was taken in for "questioning" and during the eighteen hours that she was held incommunicado, she was brutally tortured by Lindsay's finest pigs. On April 2, 1969 when fascist pig cops kicked down the door of Joan's home, she was already on $5,000. bail. This time, when she was re-arrested on the same alleged charges, she was held on a $100,000. ransom.

be used to arrest the National Leadership of the Party and other members of the New York state Chapter.

A lawsuit was filed against the N.Y.C. Department of Corrections, charging Commissioner of Corrections, George F. McGrath with being responsible for the "cruel and unusual punishment" that the N.Y. 21 are being subjected to. On October 17, 1969, after the pigs played a run around game, by changing the court-room several times, the thirteen political prisoners were brought into court, accompanied with their usual security: a-pig-a-Panther. Lying pig DA Phillips announced the new grand jury indictment, alleging that the N.Y. 21 had also conspirered to blow-up subways. This, of course was totally in-

do not make up a jury of our peer group. (point number 8 of our Platform and Program reads) WE WANT ALL BLACK PEOPLE WHEN BROUGHT TO TRIAL TO BE TRIED IN COURT BY A JURY OF THEIR PEER GROUP OR PEOPLE FROM THEIR BLACK COMMUNITY AS DEFINED BY THE CONSTITUTION OF THE UNITED STATES.

When racist pig judge Julius J. Hoffman ordered Bobby Seale, Chairman of the Black Panther Party, gagged and chained for defending his constitutional rights, and then sentenced Bobby to four years in prison for defending his rights, it became very clear that historically nothing has changed. It was Dred Scott in 1857. Now it's Bobby Seale in 1969. For in the fasicst courts of decadent America, a Black man still doesn't have any rights that a White man is born to respect.

AFENI SHAKUR

same type of Nazi justice will be used to railroad the N Y 21 off to jail when their trial starts.

Even though no trial date has been set for the Connecticut Panthers (which also has Chairman

Haven Chapter of the Party) has called for a national demonstration to protest the cruel and unusual treatment that the five Panther sisters are being subjected to (they are incarcerated at Niantic State Farm). Francis Carter, one of the three pregnant women gave birth to an eight pound baby boy on Wednesday, November 12, 1969. She named the baby, Che Alprentice(Bunchy) Carter. Rose Smith is due, interestingly enough, on December 24th or the 25th. Prison authorities have announced that the rest of the pregnant women will give birth under heavy armed guard in Lawrence Memorial Hospital in New London.

POW's FOR PANTHERS!
Zayd
Deputy Minister of Culture
N.Y.S. Chapter
Black Panther Party

SPEECH AT RALLY FOR PANTHER 21

On the eve of Friday, November 7th, in Rio Piedras, Puerto Rico, an attempt was made to burn down and destroy the national office of the Movement Pro Independence of Puerto Rico. The attack was headed by mobsters and deceased Cuban exiled worms and assisted by the colonial pigs. The attackers threw stones and tried to set fire to the building while the colonial pigs fired into the offices injuring Patriots, who, unarmed, valiantly defended their headquarters against the attackers. This attack against our brothers in the Island resounded and was felt here in New York. The Puerto Rican community, including the Puerto Rican students, assembled to denounce the political repression manifested on that eve and the day following the initial attack. Out of this assembly was born a coalition of Puerto Rican community and student groups. Today the coalition is making its first and firm stand to denounce the political repression here in the United States and in Puerto Rico.

We demand the release of all political prisoners, our brothers the Black Panthers, the Young Lords, the Puerto Rican Nationalists and our oppressed communities as well, for we are all political prisoners. If you don't understand what this means, if you think you are free, look around you. Look at the deplorable living conditions we are forced to live under. Look at the rats, the roaches, the miseducation our children receive, the permanent unemployment, the lack of adequate health programs, the degenerating welfare system that keeps our people impoverished and feeling incapable of functioning fully as a human being. Look at the drug scene that is killing our youth. Look at the migrant workers working from sunrise to sunset with one meal a day that cannot be called a meal where even the basic sanitary conditions are denied. Look at the political machinery that says it represents you and meanwhile passes laws that keep you repressed and if necessary will violate these very laws to repress you. If you don't believe that, look at what they are doing to Bobby Seale in Chicago.

In Puerto Rico Yanqui military bases occupy 30% of our able land. We are prisoners of the owners of the factories that exploit us with hunger salaries, of the rich Whites that own the cement slums where we pay the highest rents, of the racists that don't want us to have our education either in Puerto Rico's high schools or universities. We are also prisoners of the pigs that arrest us just because we are Puerto Ricans. The so-called war on poverty acts as a sucking machine to suck up our poten-

tial leadership and sets up phony programs to keep our attention diverted. Why? So we wouldn't think, and if we don't think we don't act.

The so-called justice department which we call the injustice department, has declared a war against the people. This is evident in the arrests made. Some of our brothers are jailed two, three oand four times. Some are in jail right now, inside prisons here and in Puerto Rico, just because they have struggled against this system. Pedro Albizu Campos spent half of his life in a Yanqui prison just because he protested and fought against social injustice. He was arrested, tortured and killed because he tried to destroy this system of exploitation and to build humane Puerto Rican society and nationality. Also jailed are dozens of Puerto Rican Nationalists, from our communities in New York and Chicago. Paul Luciano, Puerto Rican fighter of the Young Lords, has been arrested and imprisoned because he defended the Puerto Rican community. More than 100 brothers from the Black Panther Party, the revolutionary vanguard of the Black people, are also in jail. Today a mistrial will be held to try 21 Black Panthers. These are our people, they fight for our people. All of them have struggled with the people against exploitation.

Dick Gregory once said, "We are the convicts, but in Washington there are criminals, someday the convicts will be able to convict the criminals". We say, we are all convicts, we were born convicts and are now living the sentence. We the convicts are larger in number and the day is coming when we shall try all these criminals that are trying us now. And our trials will not be mistrials like theirs, for our trials will be trials by the people.

We the coalition of Puerto Rican community and student groups demand the release of our political prisoners. NOW

FREE THE BLACK PANTHERS
FREE THE YOUNG LORDS
FREE THE PUERTO RICAN NATIONALISTS

VIVA PUERTO RICO LIBRE
VIVA THE STRUGGLE OF THE OPPRESSED MASSES
POWER TO THE PEOPLE!

Aida Cuascot
Puerto Rican Coalition
MPI (Lucha)

FREE THE N.Y. PANTHER 21!

LEGACY

What Does This Mean to You?

"I know you are here to kill me. Shoot coward, you are only going to kill a man." - Ernesto "Che" Guevara

"Memories of the past time giving up cash to the leaders knowin' damn well they ain't gonna feed us." - Tupac Shakur

"A nation that continues year after year to spend more money on military defense than on programs of social uplift is approaching spiritual doom." - Rev. Dr. Martin Luther King, Jr.

"The life of a single human being is worth a million times more than all the property of the richest man on earth."- Ernesto "Che" Guevara

"Alcohol will make a lazy nigga slip and fall, miss his call." - Tupac Shakur

"The media is the most powerful entity on earth. They have the power to make the innocent guilty and to make the guilty innocent, and that's power; because they control the minds of the masses." - Malcolm X

"History will have to record that the greatest tragedy of this period of social transition was not the strident clamor of the bad people, but the appalling silence of the good people." - Rev. Dr. Martin Luther King, Jr.

"It is only who is thoroughly acquainted with the evils of war that can thoroughly understand the profitable way of carrying it on." - Sun Tzu, *The Art of War*

"I'm watching my nation die, genocide the cause. Expect a blood bath. The aftermath is yalls!!" - Tupac Shakur

"The basic clay of our work is the youth; we place our hope in it and prepare it to take the banner from our hands." - Ernesto "Che" Guevara

Better Dayz

Tupac Shakur, Better Dayz (Disc II)

(Hook)

Looking for those better days.

Better days, better days, better days

Thinking' about the better days

Better days, better days, better days

Got me thinking' about better days

Time to question our lifestyle, look how we all live. Smoking weed like it ain't no thing, so even kids wanna try now, they lie down and get ran through. Nobody watches and clockin' the evil men do. Faced with the demon, addicted to hearing victims screaming, guess we was evil from birth, product of cursed semen. Cause even our birthdays are cursed days. A born thug in the first place, the worst way. I'd love to see the block in peace, with no dealers and crooked cops, the only way to stop the beast. And only we can change. It's up to us to clean up the streets, it ain't the same. Too many murders, too many funerals and too many tears. Just seen another brother buried plus I knew him for years. Passed by his family but what can I say? Keep your head up and try to keep the faith for better days.

Thinking back as an adolescent, who would have guessed that in my future years, I'd be stressing. Some say the ghetto sick is and corrupted, plus my PO won't let me hang with the brothers that I grew up with. Trying to keep my head up and stay strong. All the homies slinging yayo all day long, but they wrong. So I'm solo and so broke. Saving up for some Jordan's, cause they dope. I got a girl and I love her, but she broke too, and so am I. I can't take her to the places she wanna go to. So we argue and play fight, all day and night. Making passionate love til the daylight. Plus, we about to get evicted, can't pay the rent, guess it's time to see who really is your friend. Tell me you're pregnant and I'm amazed. So many blessings while we stressing. Looking for those better days.

Now me and you was real cool, hell on them square fools. Since back in high school, we was true, me and you. Hardly parted or separated we stayed faded. Affiliated with gangbangers and still made it. Up in the gym, mess with me, gotta' mess with him. Still dressing like grown ol' men, we rollin'. Out in the dark, smoking Newport's, gamin marks, got a place in my heart, homie stay smart. Locked you up in the pen and gave you 3 to 10. I send you letters with naked flicks of old friends. Hoping you well. I know it's hell doing the time in the cell you need mail when you in jail. And me, I'm doing cool. I settled down and had a family, working and in night school. Every once in a while, I reminisce and wonder how we ever came to this. I miss the better days.

I send this out to all my homeboys down in Clinton locked down. Riker's Island, all them dudes I was locked up with. E block, F block, the lower H, NIC in Rikers Island. Down state. All the peoples that I met along the way. Better days is coming homeboy. Keep ya head up.

Let's Talk About it

This piece is a reflection on life as well as an open letter between him and a close friend. Some verses read as if it is meant to inspire us to do better and be better examples to our youth, while other verses read as a communication between long-term friends. This piece is about faith and remaining hopeful in the face of adversity. It also brings to mind the value of childhood friendships that even if faded over time, leave forever memories.

Even communities that struggle are filled with people who love each other and long for better days to come. Their hopes and dreams are just as real and important as those people born into better economic conditions, but because of stereotypical fears and a real lack of concern, it often goes unnoticed and unsupported. Is it a coincidence that the majority of guns manufactured in America make their way to the ghetto? Is it a coincidence that drugs miraculously shipped into our nation's ports make their way to the poorest neighborhoods? Is it not by design that the ghetto is where good health and education are cast aside by our nation's government? Is it not by design that the impoverished communities sit on top of the poorest land and air quality?

Ossie Davis, actor and activist, once said, "where justice is denied, where poverty is enforced, where ignorance prevails, and where any one class is made to feel that society is an organized conspiracy to oppress, rob and degrade them, neither persons nor property will be safe." It is naïve to assume there will be no repercussions for America's turning of its back on our poor and our youth.

Even with this opposition, the ghetto is full of hope and ambition. The people who live in substandard conditions are strong and mighty people who have been tested throughout time. Some will fall into the traps of addiction and violence, but others don't. Tupac wrote this song speaking to both. James Baldwin once said, "Children have never been good at listening to their elders, but they have never failed to imitate them."

It is unfathomable to expect a young mind to be able to process, in their developing brains, what behavior is acceptable for their age group and what behavior is solely for adults or is illegal, when constant media barrage glorify both things. Parents hope they weave through all of these influences and come out unaffected.

Tupac opens this song by stating, "time to question our lifestyle, look how we live. Smokin' weed like it ain't no thing, so even kids wanna try now, they lie down and get ran through. Nobody watches and clockin' the evil men do?"

Discussion

1. Does adult behavior in life or in theater affect the mindset and actions of our children?

2. Have you ever used the expression or been told, "do as I say, not as I do?"

3. Do you have a responsibility for children that you do not know and have never met?

4. Do sex, drugs, and violence on TV, social media, and cinema, play a role in child drug addiction, gangs, and teenage pregnancies?

5. What has been done in your own home to limit these risks on your children?

6. Does the availability of sex, drugs, and alcohol seem to have changed today compared to when you grew up? How will it continue to change?

Tupac describes the thought of a person by going on to write "faced with demons, addicted to hearing victims screaming, guess we was evil since birth, product of cursed semen. Cause even our birthdays are cursed days. A born thug in the first place, the worst way."

1. Can poor conditions produce good people? Are their odds the same as a child born in above standard conditions?
2. What is your idea of poverty versus your idea of wealth?
3. Can an evil environment become addictive? Consider the molested child that grows up to become a pedophile or a son that watched his mother be beaten, grows up to beat the woman in his life.
4. Put yourself in the mindset of a child born into poverty or an abusive environment. Can you understand why a child may act out in ways that are harmful to themselves or their community?
5. How bad must it be for a child to consider their own birthday as a curse day?

In a hopeful way, Tupac speaks of his aspirations in the midst of it all. He writes, "I'd love to see the block in peace. With no more dealers and crooked cops, the only way to stop the beast. And only we can change. It's up to us to clean up the streets, it ain't the same. Too many murders, too many funerals and too many tears. Just seen another brother buried plus I knew him for years. Passed by his family, but what can I say? Keep your head up and try to keep the faith. And pray for better days."

1. Can a person be a product of the drug culture and still desire peace? Is this a contradiction?
2. Can a person own several guns and be against gun violence?
3. Talk about some instances you've witnessed or experienced police racial bias. If you can't come up with any, reflect on cases you've heard of in the media.
4. Slavery was brought to the United States more than 400 years ago, enforced by all levels of law enforcement. Segregation, the same. How do these systemic ideologies end?

5. Should law enforcement be regularly trained in the vast range of racial and culture differences that make up America?

6. Do you consider Law Enforcement fair and balanced in your community?

7. What type of community programs or services can help children and families that are in high crime areas?

8. How can the government satisfy gun owner rights and also stop the increasing rate of deaths caused by guns? Can organizations like the NRA play a role?

9. Do you believe the NRA feels encouraged to take responsibility for any irresponsible use of their product?

10. Why are these kinds of organizations nonprofit?

11. Should gun manufacturers be held accountable for unlawful use of their firearms?

12. Should military-grade guns be in the hands of civilians? How will your community police force counter and protect themselves against military grade guns?

In the next verse Tupac is reflecting on his past life, talking about the consequences of previous actions while staying positive about the future. He states, "Thinking back as an adolescent, who would have guessed in my future years, I'd be stressing. Some say the ghetto is sick and corrupted, plus my PO won't let me hang with the brothers I grew up with. Trying to keep my head up and stay strong. All my homies slinging yayo all day long, but they wrong. So I am solo and so broke. Saving up for some Jordans cause they dope. I got a girl and I love her, but she broke too, and so am I. I can't take her to the places she wanna go to. So we argue and play fight, all day and night. Makin' passionate love til the daylight. Plus we about to get evicted, can't pay the rent. Guess it's really time to see who really is your friend. Tell me you're pregnant and I am amazed. So many blessings while we're stressing. Looking for those better days."

1. Can a person change when their environment stays the same?

2. Does being poor lead to committing crimes or being the victim of crimes?

3. Talk about a time when you struggled but you were able to appreciate your blessings.

4. If you had no money, what would you do to provide for yourself? Your family?

5. Should a person be judged for supporting an illegal income for the benefit of taking care of their family?

Tupac closes out this song as if he is reading a letter that has been written between two childhood friends. It sounds as if one is incarcerated; therefore, the physical nature of their friendship has been compromised, but the love and memories are alive and well. Best friends are at times the only sense of family a child may have, yet there may come a time when their paths in life take a different road. In maturing, this is inevitable. Tupac appears to be reflecting on a friendship that matured and grew apart in distance but stayed together in spirit. He states "Now me and you was real cool, hell on them square fools. Since back in high school, we was true, me and you. Hardly parted or separated, we stayed faded. Affiliated with gang members and still made it. Up in the gym, mess with me, gotta mess with him. Still dressing like old men, we rollin'. Out in the dark, smoking Newport's gamin marks, got a place in my heart, homie stayed smart. Locked you up in the pen and gave you 3 to 10. I send you letters with naked flicks of old friends. Hoping you well, I know it's hell doing time in the cell, you need mail when you in jail. And me? I'm doing cool. Settled down and had a family, working and in night school. Every once in a while, I reminisce and wonder how we ever came to this. I miss the better days."

1. Do you have a childhood friend that is or was very dear to you? How does that childhood friendship compare to friendships you made as adults?

2. Do you believe that a child affiliated with gang members is just as much a risk to society as the gang member? Do you believe that a child affiliated with supremacy gangs are just as much as risk to society as the supremacist?

3. What is your interpretation of Tupac's "affiliated"? What is the difference between being affiliated and being an active member of these groups?

4. Have you had a friend or loved one incarcerated for an extended period of time? Were you there for this person as you would have wanted he or she to be there for you?

5. What if your friend committed a heinous crime that you found extremely hard to understand or forgive; would you still physically and emotionally be there?

6. Has incarceration made people better or worse?

7. What kind of friend are you and what kind of friends do you have in your life?

8. Are you a leader or a follower? Give examples.

Life Goes On

Tupac Shakur, All Eyes On Me

How many brothers fell victim to the streets, rest in peace young nigga, there's a heaven for a G. It be a lie if I told you that I never thought of death. My nigga, we the last ones left. But life goes on. (repeat)

As I bail through the empty hall's breath stinking and my draws, ring ring ring, quiet y'all incoming call. Plus, this my homie from high school he's getting by, it's time to bury another brother nobody cries. Life as a baller alcohol and booty calls. We used to do them as adolescents, do you recall? Raised as G's, bloked out and blazed the weed, get on the rooftop let's get smoked out and blaze with me. Two in the morning and we still high assed out. Screaming thug til I die before I pass out. But now that you're gone, I'm in a zone thinking' I don't want to die all alone. But now ya gone. And all I got left are stinking' memories, I love them niggas to death, I'm drinking Hennessy while trying to make it last. I drank a 5th for your ass when you passed cause life goes on.

(Chorus)

Yeah nigga, I got the word as hell, you blew trial and the judge gave you 25 with an L. Time to prepare to do fed time won't see parole, imagine life as a convict that's getting old. Plus with the drama of looking out for your baby mama, taking risks, while keeping cheap tricks from getting on her. Life in the hood is all good for nobody. Remember gamin on dumb hotties at your parties. Me and you, no true a two, while scheming on hits and getting tricks that maybe we can slide into. But now you're buried, rest nigga, cause I aint worried, eyes blurry saying goodbye at your cemetery. Though memories fade, I got your name tatted on my arm so we both ball til my dying days. Before I say goodbye, Kato and Mento Rest in peace. Thug til I die.

Bury me smiling with G's in pocket, have party at my funeral and every rapper rock it. Let the hoes that I used to know, from way before, kiss me from my head to my toe. Give me a paper and pen so I can write about my life of sin, a couple bottles of gin in case I don't get in. Tell all my people I'm a rider, nobody cries when we die. We Outlawz let me ride! Until I get free, I live my life in the fast lane, got police chasing me. To my niggas from old blocks from old crews, niggas that guided me through back in the old school. Pour out some liquor, have a toast for the homie, see we both gotta die but you chose to go before me. And brothers miss you while you're gone, you left your nigga on his own, how long we mourn. Life Goes On.

Life goes on homie. For all the homies that have passed away. Niggas doing life. Niggas doing' 50 and 60 years and shit. I feel you Nigga, trust me, I feel you. Last year, we poured out liquor for you. This year Life Goes On. Fidna to clock now, getting money, evade bitches, evade tricks, get players plenty space. Basically just represent for you baby. The next time you see you Niggas, we gone be on top Nigga. You gone be like God damn, dem niggas came up. That's right baby. Life Goes On. We up out this bitch. Hey Kato and Mento, y'all make sure its poppin' when we get up there nigga. Don't front!

Let's Talk About it

When people think of Tupac and his music, Life Goes On probably does not immediately come to mind. Tupac speaks on topics of death and dying in the ghetto, but this time he tackles it from the griever's perspective. He isn't the only rapper to speak of grief, but he's one of few that didn't leave it to one liners and taglines. This song is a rare find because it takes you on the journey of a person feeling the loss, not just in a verse, but in full memory.

Only great writers like Tupac can entwine rhyme and rhythm within a great story that can easily be turned into a play or movie, simply because of the depth of its verses. Tupac was not just a rapper. Tupac aspired to be "more than just a rap musician," but an "elevation to today's generation if he can make them listen." He went on to say in the next verse, "prison ain't what we need, no longer stuck in greed, time to plan and strategize, our families gotta eat." It may be so that more people listened to Tupac than he could have ever imagined in his lifetime, but he knew his words would live on through his music.

Tupac opens the song telling us about a dear old friend he grew up with, who he trusted and loved. The two of them shared countless memories; childhood friendship is usually one of the most memorable relationships of a person's lifetime. Childhood is the one thing, that we hope of all things, was a good and rewarding experience for every person.

We can go on in life with the assumption that everyone's childhood was like our own. We can assume that my life experience is your life experience. Neither of these are true and both of these thoughts harm our communities and our tolerance for one another. Children should be safe, fed, clothed and loved, while also acquiring skills of compassion and empathy.

As children we should learn the way of family and friendship, how to respect authority and rely on our elders and peer's guidance. Childhood is where we learn how to play in the playground, have our first fist fight, our first kiss, and our first games of hide and seek. Our childhood, good, bad or indifferent, plays a major role in who we become.

Tupac wanted to remind us here, that every person who is murdered was someone's friend and member of community. Let's talk about this verse from the eyes of the one that is grieving.

Discussion

1. Is there a timeline for grief?

2. How do you want to be remembered? How will you be remembered?

3. Is there a death experience in your life that changed you?

4. Have you ever maintained your negative thoughts towards a person after their death? Why?

5. Have you thought of what your memory will be to others?

6. Name 5 good qualities about yourself that you want to live on forever.

7. Name 5 bad qualities about yourself you think your future grandchildren may not be happy with.

How do you want to be remembered? This is a question that drove Tupac and made him very conscious of his character and standing. He allowed us to watch him grow through life, beginning as the son of a prominent high-ranking east coast Black Panther to learning at the School of Arts in Baltimore, to living in ghettos of Long Beach, California, and other west coast neighborhoods.

We watched him perform with the Digital Underground while being an avid reader and poet. We admired his political and militant styles of his first albums and then the Thug Life stories he brought to us. We watched him changing chapters and moving into acting and outright activism. He wanted to direct and write plays so that he could be in a better position to help his community. Tupac wanted to see a better environment for his brothers and sisters to gain real economic wealth and to see that there is more than the ghetto or the bad situation that lies in front of them - life goes on.

Tupac spoke of his death often, but he was gifted and may have sensed that his time was short, or he simply took advantage of every living moment - something we should all probably do a bit more of. This piece told us how he wanted us to celebrate his life. He wrote this song as if he was smiling while considering his own death.

1. What was positive about your childhood? What was negative?

2. Do you agree with the idea that someone can love where they live but not love the experience there? Why or why not?

3. Do you know someone who had a difficult childhood? How is that person affected?

4. What is your best childhood memory?

5. What phase of your adolescence was the best?

6. What is an experience you had that you want to be sure to pass on?

7. Did you have a childhood best friend? What is that relationship like today?

What Does This Mean to You II?

"They could never understand what you set out to do. Instead, they chose to ridicule you. When you got weak, they loved the sight of your dimming and flickering starlight. How could they understand what was so intricate? To be loved by so many, so intimate, they wanted to see your lifeless corpse. This way you could not alter their course of ignorance that they have set to make people forget what they have done for much too long, to just carry on. I had loved you forever because of who you are and now I mourn, our Fallen Star." - Tupac Shakur

"Shed tears as we bury niggas close to the heart, what was a friend, now a ghost in the dark." - Tupac Shakur

"O' Lord help me be pure, but not yet." - St. Augustine

"How many caskets can we witness before we see it's hard to live this life without God. So we must ask forgiveness." - Tupac Shakur

"But what we can do, as flawed as we are, is still see God in other people, and do our best to help them find their own grace. That's what I strive to do, that's what I pray to do every day." - Barack Obama

the Black Nation is simm
hot news that the Hon
Louis Farrakhan ha
National Chairman o
Panther Party, Atto
Shabazz to be a
the Million Man
anniversary. The
ment came on J
Temple Baptist
D.C. Shabazz,
Dr. Khallid A
National Yo
Million You
the Minis
New Bla
Black
Nation
Revo
ort

FREE MALACHI Z. YORK! feature pg. 1

E NEW BLACK PANTHER

The Voice of Black Power, Revolution and the Hip-Hop Generation

VOLUME 3 NUMBER 1   MARCH / APRIL 2005

www.newblackpanther.co

MMM
X

Million Man Marc
Strikes Black!!!

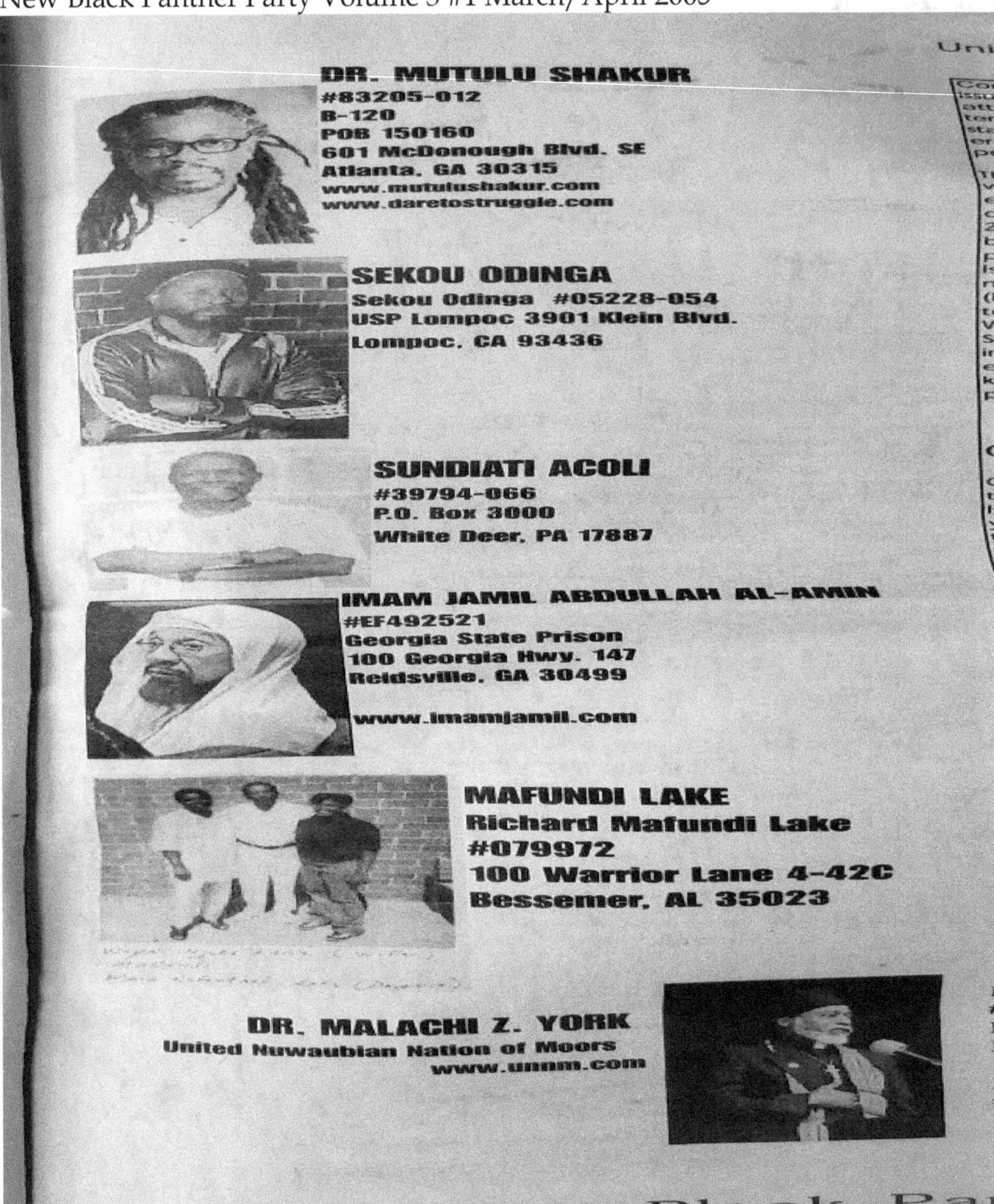
DR. MUTULU SHAKUR
#83205-012
B-120
POB 150160
601 McDonough Blvd. SE
Atlanta, GA 30315
www.mutulushakur.com
www.daretostruggle.com

SEKOU ODINGA
Sekou Odinga #05228-054
USP Lompoc 3901 Klein Blvd.
Lompoc, CA 93436

SUNDIATI ACOLI
#39794-066
P.O. Box 3000
White Deer, PA 17887

IMAM JAMIL ABDULLAH AL-AMIN
#EF492521
Georgia State Prison
100 Georgia Hwy. 147
Reidsville, GA 30499

www.imamjamil.com

MAFUNDI LAKE
Richard Mafundi Lake
#079972
100 Warrior Lane 4-42C
Bessemer, AL 35023

DR. MALACHI Z. YORK
United Nuwaubian Nation of Moors
www.unnm.com

The New Black Pa

About the Author

Desiree was born in 1971 in New Jersey, a product of the birth of the hip hop era. Born only 5 months after Tupac, she has always loved the hip hop genre and culture, and like Tupac she is also a grateful fruit that has grown from the trees the Civil Rights movement have planted. Desiree grew up a huge fan of MC Lyte and KRS-One and other groundbreaking artists of the time. She grew up in Essex County where she attended and graduated from the Montclair school system. From there Desiree went to graduate from HBCU;, Delaware State College. She later got her CPA, married, divorced, and became the proud mom of a daughter and a son.

Desiree began reading Richard Wright style books and moved onto books of the Civil Rights era as a teen. There she became captivated with all things and the people that were of the struggle for black and brown equality here in America. Woman like Afeni Shakur, Assata Shakur, Elaine Davis, to the men such as Fred Hampton, Bobby Seale, Hewey P. Newton, Mumia Abu Jamal, Martin Luther King, Malcolm X and John Lewis are underappreciated today, and she wants to keep their stories alive for the later generations that don't know them.

Desiree says, regarding this work and her connection to Tupac Shakur:

When Tupac was murdered, I grieved heavily as all the other Tupac fans. I not only grieved for the rapper, but for the son of Afeni Shakur. I grieved for a direct and hands-on product of my own Freedom Fighters. I grieved for America's loss of his intellect. I grieved for a long time and became more immersed in his music because I needed the connection. When he was alive, I feared for his life, so when he died it was quite hard to bear. I am also a confessed alive theorist - but I have since let that idea go.

As time passed, I became very disappointed and angry with the heads of the hip hop community. From successful rappers to the businessmen, I watched them honor Tupac and their love for him while at the very same time I watched Tupac's kids, The Outlaws, struggling. I couldn't reconcile the two things, and my heart always went out to my one-time homie and now deceased Bruce Washington - AKA Fatal from the Outlaws - Kadafi, and the rest of his bandmates who were all local dope artists. These young guys were talented, and I felt like the rap industry failed them. I don't know all backstories, so pardon me for anyone that I have offended, but it's how I've felt.

I write this as a scholarly tool and workbook, using his voice and my own so that these types of dialogue can continue to grow Tupac's legacy in a manner that makes his love for each of us worthwhile. I write this book to contribute to the legacy of Tupac Shakur through licensing and royalty share agreements. Tupac said he may not change the world, but he may spark the brain of the person that changes the world. Let's continue to spark some brains and further Tupac Shakur's legacy in a manner in which his elders and our future generations can live as healthy, respected people that live and walk in peace and love of our differences instead of the fear of the same.

With all my Respect and Love,

Desiree

Copyright

All rights reserved.   No part of this publication may be reproduced, distributed, or transmitted in any form or by any means, including photocopying, recording, or other electronic or mechanical methods, without the prior written permission of the author and the publisher, except in the case of brief quotations embodied in critical reviews and certain noncommercial uses permitted copyright law. For permission request, write to the author.

Certificate of Registration; Let's Talk About It TXu-2-311-962
ISBN # 9798362038595

Krazy

Words and Music by Tupac Shakur, Yafeu Fula, Katari Cox, Muta Beale, Rufus Lee Cooper and Tyrone Wrice
Copyright © 2002 UNIVERSAL MUSIC CORP., AMARU PUBLISHING, YAKI KADAFI MUSIC, KATARI COX PUBLISHING DESIGNEE,

MUTA BEALE PUBLISHING DESIGNEE, RUFUS LEE COOPER PUBLISHING DESIGNEE and TYRONE WRICE PUBLISHING DESIGNEE

All Rights for AMARU PUBLISHING and YAKI KADAFI MUSIC Administered by UNIVERSAL MUSIC CORP.

All Rights Reserved Used by Permission

Reprinted by permission of Hal Leonard LLC

White Man'z World
Words and Music by Tupac Shakur and Marvin Harper
Copyright © 1996 SONGS OF UNIVERSAL, INC., JOSHUA'S DREAM MUSIC and SUGE
    PUBLISHING
All Rights for JOSHUA'S DREAM MUSIC Controlled and Administered by SONGS OF UNIVERSAL,
    INC.
All Rights Reserved   Used by Permission
Reprinted by permission of Hal Leonard LLC

My Block
Words and Music by Tupac Shakur, Christopher Howard Jasper, Marvin Isley, Ernest Isley, O. Kelly Jr
Isley, Rudolph Isley, Osten S. Jr Harvey and Ronald Isley
Copyright © 1995 EMI April Music Inc., Bovina Music Inc., Universal Music Corp. and Amaru Publishing
All Rights on behalf of EMI April Music Inc. and Bovina Music Inc. Administered by Sony Music
Publishing (US) LLC, 424 Church Street, Suite 1200, Nashville, TN 37219
All Rights on behalf of Amaru Publishing Administered by Universal Music Corp.
International Copyright Secured   All Rights Reserved
Reprinted by permission of Hal Leonard LLC

Me Against The World
Words and Music by Tupac Shakur, Yafeu Fula, Malcolm Greenidge, Leon Ware, Minnie Riperton, Richard
Rudolph, Burt Bacharach, Hal David, Carsten Schack and Kenneth Karlin
Copyright © 1995 UNIVERSAL MUSIC CORP., AMARU PUBLISHING, YAKI KADAFI MUSIC,
FOXBEAT MUSIC, NEW HIDDEN VALLEY MUSIC CO., PW ARRANGEMENTS, EMI
BLACKWOOD MUSIC INC., SOULVANG MUSIC, EMBASSY MUSIC CORPORATION,
JOBETE MUSIC CO., INC., DICKIEBIRD MUSIC, CASA DAVID and FULL OF SOUL MUSIC
All Rights for AMARU PUBLISHING, YAKI KADAFI MUSIC, FOXBEAT MUSIC, NEW HIDDEN
VALLEY MUSIC CO. and PW ARRANGEMENTS Administered by UNIVERSAL MUSIC CORP.
All Rights for EMI BLACKWOOD MUSIC INC. and SOULVANG MUSIC Administered by SONY
MUSIC PUBLISHING (US) LLC, 424 Church Street, Suite 1200, Nashville, TN 37219
All Rights for JOBETE MUSIC CO., INC. and DICKIEBIRD MUSIC Controlled and Administered by
EMBASSY MUSIC CORPORATION
All Rights for FULL OF SOUL MUSIC Administered by SONGS OF KOBALT MUSIC PUBLISHING
All Rights Reserved   Used by Permission
Reprinted by permission of Hal Leonard LLC

Hail Mary
Words by Tupac Shakur, Rufus Cooper, Katari Cox, Yafeu Fula, Joseph Paquette, Bruce Washington and
Tyrone Wrice
Music by Tyrone Wrice
Copyright © 1996 UNIVERSAL MUSIC CORP., YAKI KADAFI MUSIC, FOXBEAT MUSIC, AMARU
PUBLISHING, SONGS OF UNIVERSAL, INC., GIMME MINZ PUBLISHING, ROYAL SAFARI
MUSIC and TYRONE WRICE PUBLISHING DESIGNEE
All Rights for YAKI KADAFI MUSIC, FOXBEAT MUSIC and AMARU PUBLISHING Administered by
UNIVERSAL MUSIC CORP.
All Rights for GIMME MINZ PUBLISHING and ROYAL SAFARI MUSIC Administered by SONGS OF
UNIVERSAL, INC.
All Rights Reserved   Used by Permission
Reprinted by permission of Hal Leonard LLC

Military Minds
Words and Music by Tupac Shakur, Darrell Yates, Kenyatta Blake, Marvin Harper and Tekomin Williams
Copyright © 2002 UNIVERSAL MUSIC CORP., AMARU PUBLISHING, DARRELL YATES
    PUBLISHING DESIGNEE, KENYATTA BLAKE PUBLISHING DESIGNEE, MARVIN HARPER
    PUBLISHING DESIGNEE and TEKOMIN WILLIAMS PUBLISHING DESIGNEE
All Rights for AMARU PUBLISHING Administered by UNIVERSAL MUSIC CORP.
All Rights Reserved   Used by Permission
Reprinted by permission of Hal Leonard LLC

Fame
Words and Music by Tupac Shakur, Yafeu Fula, Katari Cox, Muta Beale, Rufus Lee Cooper and Tyrone
    Wrice
Copyright © 2002 UNIVERSAL MUSIC CORP., AMARU PUBLISHING, YAKI KADAFI MUSIC,
    KATARI COX PUBLISHING DESIGNEE, MUTA BEALE PUBLISHING DESIGNEE, RUFUS
    LEE COOPER PUBLISHING DESIGNEE and TYRONE WRICE PUBLISHING DESIGNEE
All Rights for AMARU PUBLISHING and YAKI KADAFI MUSIC Administered by UNIVERSAL
    MUSIC CORP.
All Rights Reserved   Used by Permission
Reprinted by permission of Hal Leonard LLC

Better Dayz
Words and Music by Tupac Shakur, Christopher Howard Jasper, Marvin Isley, Ernest Isley, O. Kelly Jr
    Isley, Rudolph Isley, Ronald Isley, Johnny Lee Jackson and Tyruss Gerald Himes
Copyright © 2002 EMI April Music Inc., Bovina Music Inc., Universal Music Corp., Amaru Publishing,
    Universal Music - MGB Songs, Black Hispanic Music, Universal Music - Z Tunes LLC and Imperial
    Loco Ent.
All Rights on behalf of EMI April Music Inc. and Bovina Music Inc. Administered by Sony Music
    Publishing (US) LLC, 424 Church Street, Suite 1200, Nashville, TN 37219
All Rights on behalf of Amaru Publishing Administered by Universal Music Corp.
All Rights on behalf of Black Hispanic Music Administered by Universal Music - MGB Songs
All Rights on behalf of Imperial Loco Ent. Administered by Universal Music - Z Tunes LLC
International Copyright Secured   All Rights Reserved
Reprinted by permission of Hal Leonard LLC

Life Goez On
Words and Music by Tupac Shakur, Johnny Jackson, Joseph Jefferson, Charles Simmons and Stacey Smallie
Copyright © 1996 UNIVERSAL MUSIC CORP., AMARU PUBLISHING, UNIVERSAL MUSIC - MGB
      SONGS, JOSEPH JEFFERSON PUBLISHING DESIGNEE, CHARLES SIMMONS PUBLISHING
      DESIGNEE and STACEY SMALLIE PUBLISHING DESIGNEE
All Rights for AMARU PUBLISHING Administered by UNIVERSAL MUSIC CORP.
All Rights Reserved   Used by Permission
Reprinted by permission of Hal Leonard LLC

Nice
Words and Music by Beyonce Knowles, Pharrell Williams, Shawn Carter, Denisia Andrews and Brittany
      Coney
Copyright © 2018 Oakland 13 Music, EMI Pop Music Publishing, More Water From Nazareth, Carter Boys
      Music, Denisia Andrews Publishing Designee and Brittany Coney Publishing Designee
All Rights on behalf of Oakland 13 Music, EMI Pop Music Publishing, More Water From Nazareth and
      Carter Boys Music Administered by Sony Music Publishing (US) LLC, 424 Church Street, Suite
      1200, Nashville, TN 37219
International Copyright Secured   All Rights Reserved
Reprinted by permission of Hal Leonard LLC

Unconditional Love
Words and Music by Tupac Shakur and Johnny Jackson
Copyright © 1998 UNIVERSAL MUSIC CORP., AMARU PUBLISHING and UNIVERSAL MUSIC –
      MGB SONGS
All Rights for AMARU PUBLISHING Administered by UNIVERSAL MUSIC CORP.
All Rights Reserved   Used by Permission
Reprinted by permission of Hal Leonard LLC

Ambitionz Az A Ridah
Words and Music by Tupac Shakur and Delmar Arnaud
Copyright © 1996 UNIVERSAL MUSIC CORP., AMARU PUBLISHING and DELMAR ARNAUD
      PUBLISHING DESIGNEE
All Rights for AMARU PUBLISHING Administered by UNIVERSAL MUSIC CORP.
All Rights Reserved   Used by Permission
Reprinted by permission of Hal Leonard LLC

To Live And Die In L.A.
Words and Music by Quincy Jones III, Val Young and Tupac Shakur
Copyright © 1996 by DEEP TECHNOLOGY MUSIC, MUSIC OF WINDSWEPT, UNIVERSAL MUSIC
      CORP., AMARU PUBLISHING and VAL YOUNG PUBLISHING
All Rights for DEEP TECHNOLOGY MUSIC and MUSIC OF WINDSWEPT Administered by BMG
      RIGHTS MANAGEMENT (US) LLC
All Rights for AMARU PUBLISHING Administered by UNIVERSAL MUSIC CORP.
All Rights Reserved   Used by Permission
Reprinted by permission of Hal Leonard LLC

Me Against The World
Words and Music by Tupac Shakur, Yafeu Fula, Malcolm Greenidge, Leon Ware, Minnie Riperton, Richard Rudolph, Burt Bacharach, Hal David, Carsten Schack and Kenneth Karlin
Copyright © 1995 UNIVERSAL MUSIC CORP., AMARU PUBLISHING, YAKI KADAFI MUSIC, FOXBEAT MUSIC, NEW HIDDEN VALLEY MUSIC CO., PW ARRANGEMENTS, EMI BLACKWOOD MUSIC INC., SOULVANG MUSIC, EMBASSY MUSIC CORPORATION, JOBETE MUSIC CO., INC., DICKIEBIRD MUSIC, CASA DAVID and FULL OF SOUL MUSIC
All Rights for AMARU PUBLISHING, YAKI KADAFI MUSIC, FOXBEAT MUSIC, NEW HIDDEN VALLEY MUSIC CO. and PW ARRANGEMENTS Administered by UNIVERSAL MUSIC CORP.
All Rights for EMI BLACKWOOD MUSIC INC. and SOULVANG MUSIC Administered by SONY MUSIC PUBLISHING (US) LLC, 424 Church Street, Suite 1200, Nashville, TN 37219
All Rights for JOBETE MUSIC CO., INC. and DICKIEBIRD MUSIC Controlled and Administered by EMBASSY MUSIC CORPORATION
All Rights for FULL OF SOUL MUSIC Administered by SONGS OF KOBALT MUSIC PUBLISHING
All Rights Reserved   Used by Permission
Reprinted by permission of Hal Leonard LLC

Brenda's Got A Baby
Words and Music by Deon Evans and Tupac Shakur
Copyright © 1991 UNIVERSAL MUSIC CORP., UNIVERSAL - Z SONGS and BACK ON POINT MUSIC
All Rights for BACK ON POINT MUSIC Controlled and Administered by UNIVERSAL - Z SONGS
All Rights Reserved   Used by Permission
Reprinted by permission of Hal Leonard LLC

Sound Of Da Police
Words and Music by Rodney Lemay, Lawrence Parker, Eric Burdon, Bryan Chandler and Alan Lomax
Copyright © 1993 LONDON MUSIC U.K., UNIVERSAL MUSIC - Z TUNES LLC and SLAMINA MUSIC LTD.
All Rights for LONDON MUSIC U.K. Administered by UNIVERSAL - POLYGRAM INTERNATIONAL PUBLISHING, INC.
All Rights for SLAMINA MUSIC LTD. Administered by CARLIN MUSIC CORP.
All Rights Reserved   Used by Permission
- contains elements of "Inside Looking Out (Rosie)" Words and Music by Eric Burdon, Alan Lomax and Bryan Chandler
Reprinted by permission of Hal Leonard LLC

They Don't Give A Fuck About Us
Words and Music by Tupac Shakur, Mutah Beale, Katari Cox, Yafeu Fula, Malcolm Greenidge and Johnny Jackson
Copyright © 2002 UNIVERSAL MUSIC CORP., AMARU PUBLISHING, YAKI KADAFI MUSIC and UNIVERSAL MUSIC - MGB SONGS
All Rights for AMARU PUBLISHING and YAKI KADAFI MUSIC Administered by UNIVERSAL MUSIC CORP.
All Rights Reserved   Used by Permission
Reprinted by permission of Hal Leonard LLC

Thugz Mansion (7 Remix)
Words by Tupac Shakur and Anthony Cornelius Hamilton
Music by Johnny Lee Jackson and Seven Marcus Aurelius
Copyright © 2002 UNIVERSAL MUSIC CORP., AMARU PUBLISHING, UNIVERSAL MUSIC - MGB
      SONGS, BLACK HISPANIC MUSIC, SONGS OF UNIVERSAL, INC., TAPPY WHYTE'S
      MUSIC and MARCUS AURELIUS MUSIC
All Rights for AMARU PUBLISHING Administered by UNIVERSAL MUSIC CORP.
All Rights for BLACK HISPANIC MUSIC Administered by UNIVERSAL MUSIC - MGB SONGS
All Rights for TAPPY WHYTE'S MUSIC Administered by SONGS OF UNIVERSAL, INC.
All Rights for MARCUS AURELIUS MUSIC Administered by RESERVOIR MEDIA MANAGEMENT,
      INC.
All Rights Reserved   Used by Permission
Reprinted by permission of Hal Leonard LLC

Formation
Words and Music by Beyonce Knowles, Michael Williams, Aaquil Brown, Khalif Brown and Asheton
      Hogan
Copyright © 2016 Oakland 13 Music, Warner-Tamerlane Publishing Corp., Eardrummers Entertainment
      LLC, Aaquil Brown BMI Pub Designee, Khalif Brown BMI Pub Designee, Asheton Hogan BMI Pub
      Designee, WC Music Corp. and Sounds From Eardrummers
All Rights on behalf of Oakland 13 Music Administered by Sony Music Publishing (US) LLC, 424 Church
      Street, Suite 1200, Nashville, TN 37219
All Rights on behalf of Eardrummers Entertainment LLC, Aaquil Brown BMI Pub Designee, Khalif Brown
      BMI Pub Designee and Asheton Hogan BMI Pub Designee Administered by Warner-Tamerlane
      Publishing Corp.
All Rights on behalf of Sounds From Eardrummers Administered by WC Music Corp.
International Copyright Secured   All Rights Reserved
Reprinted by permission of Hal Leonard LLC

FORMATION
Words and Music by MIKE WILL, KHALIF BROWN, ASHETON HOGAN, BEYONCE KNOWLES and AAQUIL BROWN
© 2016 WARNER-TAMERLANE PUBLISHING CORP., KHALIF BROWN BMI PUB DESIGNEE, EARDRUMMERS
ENTERTAINMENT LLC, AAQUIL BROWN BMI PUB DESIGNEE, ASHETON HOGHAN BMI PUB DESIGNEE, SOUNDS
FROM EARDRUMMERS LLC and CO-PUBLISHER(S)
All Rights on behalf of SOUNDS FROM EARDRUMMERS LLC Administered by WC MUSIC CORP.
All Rights on behalf of Itself, KHALIF BROWN BMI PUB DESIGNEE, EEARDRUMMERS ENTERTAINMENT LLC,
AAQUIL BROWN BMI PUB DESIGNEE and ASHETON HOGHAN BMI PUB DESIGNEE Administered by WARNER-
TAMERLANE PUBLISHING CORP.
All Rights Reserved
Used by Permission of ALFRED MUSIC

Say Hello
Words and Music by Shawn Carter, Tom Brocker and Aldrin Davis
Copyright © 2007 Carter Boys Music, Unichappell Music Inc., SA-Vette Music and Aldrin Davis BMI Pub
      Designee
All Rights on behalf of Carter Boys Music Administered by Sony Music Publishing (US) LLC, 424 Church
      Street, Suite 1200, Nashville, TN 37219
All Rights on behalf of SA-Vette Music Administered by Unichappell Music Inc.
All Rights on behalf of Aldrin Davis BMI Pub Designee Administered by Warner-Tamerlane Publishing
      Corp.
International Copyright Secured   All Rights Reserved
Reprinted by permission of Hal Leonard LLC

SAY HELLO
Words and Music by SHAWN CARTER, ALDRIN DAVIS and TOM BROCK
© 2007 SA-VETTE MUSIC, UNICHAPPELL MUSIC INC., ALDRIN DAVIS BMI PUB DESIGNEE and CO-PUBLISHER(S)
All Rights on behalf of Itself and A-VETTE MUSIC Administered by UNICHAPPELL MUSIC INC.
All rights on behalf of ALDRIN DAVIS BMI PUB DESIGNEE Administered by WARNER-TAMERLANE PUBLISHING CORP.
All Rights Reserved
Used by Permission of ALFRED MUSIC

Blasphemy
Words and Music by Tupac Shakur, Joseph Paquette and Tyrone J. Wrice
Copyright © 1996 UNIVERSAL MUSIC CORP., AMARU PUBLISHING, ROYAL SAFARI MUSIC and
    TYRONE J. WRICE PUBLISHING DESIGNEE
All Rights for AMARU PUBLISHING Administered by UNIVERSAL MUSIC CORP.
All Rights for ROYAL SAFARI MUSIC Administered by SONGS OF UNIVERSAL, INC.
All Rights Reserved   Used by Permission
Reprinted by permission of Hal Leonard LLC

Smile
Words and Music by Tupac Shakur, Brad Jordan, Mike Dean, Terry Lewis and James Harris
Copyright © 1997 UNIVERSAL MUSIC CORP., AMARU PUBLISHING, N-THE-WATER PUBLISHING
    INC., STILL-N-THE-WATER PUBLISHING, TERRY LEWIS PUBLISHING DESIGNEE and
    JAMES HARRIS PUBLISHING DESIGNEE
All Rights for AMARU PUBLISHING Administered by UNIVERSAL MUSIC CORP.
All Rights for N-THE-WATER PUBLISHING INC. Administered by WC MUSIC CORP.
All Rights for STILL-N-THE-WATER PUBLISHING Administered by WARNER-TAMERLANE
    PUBLISHING CORP.
All Rights Reserved   Used by Permission
Reprinted by permission of Hal Leonard LLC

SMILE
Words and Music by TUPAC SHAKUR, MIKE DEAN, BRAD JORDAN, JIMMY JAM and TERRY LEWIS
© 1997 N-THE-WATER PUBLISHING INC., STILL-N-THE-WATER PUBLISHING and CO-PUBLISHER(S)
All Rights on behalf of N-THE-WATER PUBLISHING INC. administered by WC MUSIC CORP.
All Rights on behalf of STILL-N-THE-WATER PUBLISHING Administered by WARNER-TAMERLANE PUBLISHING CORP.
All Rights Reserved
Used by Permission of ALFRED MUSIC

Who Do You Believe In
Words and Music by Tupac Shakur, Jason Kay, Toby Smith, Johnny Lee Jackson, Yafeu A. Fula and Dwight
    Delemond Williams
Copyright © 1999 Sony Music Publishing (UK) Ltd., EMI Music Publishing Ltd., Universal Music Corp.,
    Amaru Publishing, Yaki Kadafi Music, Universal Music - MGB Songs, Black Hispanic Music and
    Dwight Delemond Williams Publishing Designee
All Rights on behalf of Sony Music Publishing (UK) Ltd. and EMI Music Publishing Ltd. Administered by
    Sony Music Publishing (US) LLC, 424 Church Street, Suite 1200, Nashville, TN 37219
All Rights on behalf of Amaru Publishing and Yaki Kadafi Music Administered by Universal Music Corp.
All Rights on behalf of Black Hispanic Music Administered by Universal Music - MGB Songs
International Copyright Secured   All Rights Reserved
Reprinted by permission of Hal Leonard LLC

Hold Ya Head
Words by Tupac Shakur
Music by Tyrone Wrice
Copyright © 1996 UNIVERSAL MUSIC CORP., AMARU PUBLISHING and TYRONE WRICE
     PUBLISHING DESIGNEE
All Rights for AMARU PUBLISHING Administered by UNIVERSAL MUSIC CORP.
All Rights Reserved   Used by Permission
Reprinted by permission of Hal Leonard LLC

Dedication
Words and Music by Ermias Asghedom, Larrance Dopson, Axel Morgan, John Groover Jr., Kendrick
     Lamar, Lamar Edwards, Michael Ray Cox Jr., Alexandria Dopson and Jaire Lewis
Copyright © 2018 Sony Music Publishing (US) LLC, Peermusic III, Ltd., Songs Of Volume Ventures, Blue
     Nike Publishing, Axel Morgan Publishing Designee, John Groover Jr. Publishing Designee, Kendrick
     Lamar Publishing Designee, Lamar Edwards Publishing Designee, Michael Ray Cox Jr. Publishing
     Designee and Jaire Lewis Publishing Designee
All Rights on behalf of Sony Music Publishing (US) LLC Administered by Sony Music Publishing (US)
     LLC, 424 Church Street, Suite 1200, Nashville, TN 37219
All Rights for Songs Of Volume Ventures and Blue Mike Publishing Administered by Peermusic III, Ltd.
International Copyright Secured   All Rights Reserved
Reprinted by permission of Hal Leonard LLC

DEDICATION
Words and Music by AXEL MORGAN, ALEXANDRIA DOPSON, JOHN WESLEY GROOVER, J LEWIS, ERMAIS
ASGHEDOM, LAMAR EDWARDS, KENDRICK LAMAR and MALIK COX
© 2018 WC MUSIC CORP., HARD WORKING BLACK FOLKS INC., TOP DAWG MUSIC, AXEL MORGAN MUSIC,
WARNER-TAMERLANE PUBLISHING CORP., KENDRICK LAMAR ASCAP PUB DESIGNEE and CO-PUBLISHER(S)
All Rights on behalf of Itself, HARD WORKING BLACK FOLKS INC., TOP DAWG MUSIC and KENDRICK LAMAR
ASCAP PUB DESIGNEE Aadministered by WC MUSIC CORP.
All Rights on behalf of Itself and AXEL MORGAN MUSIC Administered by WARNER-TAMERLANE PUBLISHING
CORP.
All Rights Reserved
Used by Permission of ALFRED MUSIC

OODLES O' NOODLES BABIES
Words and Music by ANTONIO JIMENEZ, ROBERT WILLIAMS and CLARENCE SCARBOROUGH
© 2019 FOREVER RICH, ALEXSCAR MUSIC, WC MUSIC CORP., MUSIC AND DREAMS PUBLISHING and CO-
PUBLISHER(S)
All Rights on behalf of Itself, FOREVER RICH, and MUSIC AND DREAMS PUBLISHING Administered by WC MUSIC
CORP.
All Rights on behalf of ALEXSCAR MUSIC Administered by WARNER-TAMERLANE PUBLISHING CORP.
All Rights Reserved
Used by Permission of ALFRED MUSIC

OODLES O' NOODLES BABIES
Words and Music by ANTONIO JIMENEZ, ROBERT WILLIAMS and CLARENCE SCARBOROUGH
© 2019 FOREVER RICH, ALEXSCAR MUSIC, WC MUSIC CORP., MUSIC AND DREAMS PUBLISHING and CO-
PUBLISHER(S)
All Rights on behalf of Itself, FOREVER RICH, and MUSIC AND DREAMS PUBLISHING Administered by WC MUSIC
CORP.
All Rights on behalf of ALEXSCAR MUSIC Administered by WARNER-TAMERLANE PUBLISHING CORP.
All Rights Reserved
Used by Permission of ALFRED MUSIC
For the ULTRA MUSIC 15% Control Only

www.ingramcontent.com/pod-product-compliance
Lightning Source LLC
Chambersburg PA
CBHW060513120726
48002CB00011B/3141